The Boy i

# The Boy in the Attic

The Chilling, Real-Life Story of a Satanic
Murder and the Truth That Haunts

## DAVID MALONE

MAINSTREAM
PUBLISHING

EDINBURGH AND LONDON

First published in Great Britain in 2011 by
MAINSTREAM PUBLISHING COMPANY
(EDINBURGH) LTD
7 Albany Street
Edinburgh EH1 3UG

ISBN 9781780575292

A catalogue record for this book is available
from the British Library

Penguin Random House is committed to a sustainable future for
our business, our readers and our planet. This book is made from
Forest Stewardship Council® certified paper.

MIX
Paper from
responsible sources
FSC® C018179

Printed and bound in Great Britain by Clays Ltd, Elcograf S.p.A.

3 5 7 9 10 8 6 4 2

To all who have loved
and to those who can forgive.

# Acknowledgements

This book was built with tea. Lots of it. The story in the pages
that follow is told largely from the insights gained in many spoken
interviews, both on and off the record. Where possible real names
are used; a small number of witnesses asked that their names not
be included. Without the testimony of each one of these people,
this book would never have been completed. Thank you all.

As this is my first book, I have sought guidance from a range of
people more expert in the business of publishing than myself: Bill
Campbell at Mainstream Publishing, who commissioned *The Boy
in the Attic*; his editorial co-ordinator, Graeme Blaikie, who
steered me through the many hoops involved; and also publicists
Fiona Atherton and Declan Heeney for ensuring that this story
reaches the widest possible audience. Six months ago I did not
know what a literary agent does. Now I do. Thanks to Patricia
and Yvonne at Prizeman & Kinsella for their continued support.

I am forever indebted to my researcher, Sara Malone, whose
damning – yet word perfect – criticism of my first draft made me
write it again. Sara's insight and analysis are on every page of this
book. It would be a far poorer read without her work and I know
her skills will be put to great use by other authors in the future.

I have never met Eleanor Collins, who edited the final draft,
though I did briefly talk to her delightful two-year-old daughter
on the phone. It is a pity that modern communications can so
effectively remove the need for face-to-face meetings. However, if

her personality is as sharp as her editing, Eleanor is truly a bright spark. I'm sure we'll meet someday and I look forward to it.

A few people asked hard editorial questions at the outset of this project and, in doing so, set it on its way. Dr Betty Moran, an octogenarian retired GP who lives in the area where the events in *The Boy in the Attic* took place, has probed the story to its core, taking it down some unexpected alleyways. Undercover journalist Donal MacIntyre and his brother, BBC TV *Panorama* reporter Darragh, know a good story when they see one and provided encouragement all the way. Their sister, psychologist Dr Deirdre MacIntyre, offered useful insight and is quoted in the book. In Dublin, factual television producer Adrian Lynch encouraged me to dig further when I first came across this extraordinary case, and for that I am grateful. Niall Meehan, head of journalism at Griffith College in Dublin, has offered wise counsel throughout, as have journalist Fionuala Boyd, media lawyer Paul Tweed and documentary cameraman David Barker.

Quoted material outside of interviews is sourced within the text, except for Kenneth Bale's letters, which are held in the *Irish Times* archive. Lyrics for 'The Helicopter Song' appear by kind permission of Brian Warfield and The Wolfe Tones. I have briefly drawn from Darius Whelan's book *Mental Health Law and Practice*, and online publications by Jacob V. Lanning, formerly supervisory special agent at the Behavioral Science Unit within the US National Center for the Analysis of Violent Crime. The ages of criminal responsibility quoted in the final chapter are from country reports of the UNICEF Committee on the Rights of the Child. I interviewed Bobby Cummines, former bank robber and now chief executive of Unlock, an association of ex-offenders, and sourced additional material from an interview he gave to *The Guardian* on 2 February 2001. Nessa O'Connor's *Palmerstown: An Ancient Place* is a well-researched local history book which helped me to better understand the village.

Close friends who have encouraged the writing of this book include Paul McGuigan at BBC Drama, and Stuart Switzer and

Linda Cullen at Coco Television. In addition many colleagues at RTÉ and the BBC have willingly given of their time. I am also grateful to Helen, Leo, Anthony, Fiona, Cúán, Hilary, Trisha, Mary, Ameera, Jonathan, Sushila, John, Sanchia, Mark, Neil, Susan, David, Róisín, Joris, Jill, Gemma, Joe, Elizabeth, Ian, Sharon, Ceoladh and Stevie. My daughters, Sara, Kerry and Cathleen, have followed every twist of this extraordinary story with interest.

Finally, the day after I completed the manuscript, Catherine Munro walked down the aisle with me in a small church in Dublin and said 'I do'. Without her patience, love and understanding, I would never have completed this book on time, so would have brought my laptop on honeymoon. For that alone I am forever grateful.

David Malone, autumn 2011

# Contents

A Note to the Reader     13

Beginnings     17

**Chapter One**   The Boy in the Attic     21

**Chapter Two**   Love thy Neighbour     43

**Chapter Three** Thick as Thieves     65

**Chapter Four** The Shrine     97

**Chapter Five**   Penal Servitude for Life     121

**Chapter Six**     Nobody Comes into the World this Broken     155

**Chapter Seven** The 38-Year Inquest     175

**Chapter Eight**   Forgive Us Those who Trespass Against Us     193

# A Note to the Reader

*The Boy in the Attic* is a work of non-fiction and, as incredible and tragic as parts of this story are, every page documents real events.

I first learned of John Horgan's terrible murder when reading a tiny newspaper report: one short paragraph buried in the inside pages of, not an Irish paper, but a Canadian daily. I could never have imagined that this humble report would be all that the world knew of these broad-reaching, dark, strange events – events much stranger than anyone could possibly have guessed from the bare smattering of words they had been granted in the newspapers of the day.

Uncovering the truth of what happened on 14 June 1973 was not easy. Not only was the murder barely reported at the time, the few, thin accounts that had been published were inaccurate and entirely missing many key, crucial facts. Finding the full story has been a long, difficult and at times frustrating task. It would not have been possible at all without the testimony of those people with direct recall of the case. In journalism, the practice of gathering disparate pieces of information and analysing how they might fit together is known as 'collecting string'. I learned that this was a case with many defects: material evidence was removed from the crime scene by a senior Church cleric; the inquest into the death of the boy was finally completed more than three decades after the murder as a direct result of my investigations;

and a question mark still rests over why the killer's punishment appears not to fit the crime.

I could not tell this story without also conjuring the time and place in which it happened, and '70s Ireland was a very different country to today's progressive European nation. Some readers will find this book sparks vivid memories of a lost era; other, perhaps younger, readers may find the landscape very unfamiliar indeed.

For the wider world, there are lessons to be learned from this tragedy, most importantly about the need to notice the warning signs and act when a child's behaviour deviates from the norm. Children are capable of great love, the most tender gift to any family. But, in a few rare cases, they can also be guilty of great trespass – in this case, the ultimate trespass: murder. I am the father of three beautiful daughters, now fine young adults, and I was fortunate to raise them at a time when the need to understand and nurture young minds was beginning to be properly understood and to infiltrate parenting culture. Today we are generally better at talking with our children than in previous generations; the attitude that children should be 'seen but not heard' has thankfully become outdated. The question of whether the warning signs in this tragic case were missed in 1973 is discussed in later chapters, however, I firmly believe that today's child protection culture assists us all in detecting such signs.

Finally and most importantly, before beginning the telling of this story, I would like to mention the victim's family. Though the Horgans are aware this book is being written, it was not initiated by them – and nor, indeed, was it welcomed. We have exchanged respectful letters, and though they did not wish to be interviewed, I have spoken with a number of people familiar with them, then and now, and received an overwhelming impression of a remarkable couple, *good* people in every sense of the word, whose conduct at the time of the murder showed a level of Christian compassion surely beyond the capacity of most people.

\*

The writing of this book has been a remarkable journey, and the story is one that I hope you, the reader, will find as fascinating and compelling as I do.

# Beginnings

As a television producer with a long track record of making crime documentaries, I can safely say I know my murders. This is not a boast of which I am overly proud; it just goes with the territory. I have met several killers (including a number associated with the Northern Ireland conflict), and their most surprising characteristic is their ordinariness. The man whose trolley bumps into us at the supermarket might years earlier have stabbed his lover to death, yet he will show no outward sign of his crime. This normality, I believe, is at the core of our interest in the mind of a killer.

Just before Christmas 2010 I was working with an Irish television production company, considering some ideas for future documentaries. One thought, which sadly never advanced much beyond first base, sent me on an Internet newspaper search for historic Irish murders, beginning in 1960. There were a number of killings reported in the '60s, some associated with Northern Ireland, and others that had already been well documented so were of little interest to today's audience. Working in sequence through each month, I was drawn to a small article on a page largely devoted to the shipping news in, of all places, the *Montreal Gazette*. The paper's date was 18 June 1973.

'YOUTH CHARGED WITH MURDER AFTER BOY, 7, CRUCIFIED' was the headline. The article continued:

Dublin (UPI Agency). Police reported Saturday the arrest of

a 16-year-old youth as a suspect in the slaying of a 7-year-old boy found crucified on the rafters of a neighbor's (*sic*) attic. Officers identified the victim as John Horgan of Palmerstown, County Dublin. He was found dead Thursday night in the attic of a neighbor's (*sic*) home several hours after his father Terry Horgan alerted police that his son was missing. Police engaged in the search found the boy's nude and battered body with the help of tracker dogs.

'The body was nailed by the hands to the attic rafters in a crude form of crucifixion,' a police spokesman said. 'It was a pretty sickening sight.'

Initially it did not occur to me that the murder had taken place in Dublin, Ireland. This was simply because I had never heard of the case – 'crucifixion' is not a word that is easily forgotten. After making a few calls it was clear my journalist colleagues were equally uninformed. The consensus was that if such a bizarre murder had indeed taken place in Dublin, it would be well known as one of the darker chapters in the nation's history. Finding this disturbing account in a Canadian newspaper with no links to any of the Irish papers suggested that perhaps this was not an Irish story at all, that the killing may have happened in Dublin, Québec, which is a tiny district a few miles west of Montreal. Could this French-speaking suburb have been the site of this shocking killing back in 1973?

This theory quickly proved a dead end, so I took a walk through historic Georgian Dublin to the National Library of Ireland, next to the Irish parliament building in Kildare Street. The National Library is a treasured institution where, given enough time, one can discover just about anything concerning Ireland's history. The expert staff pulled out rolls of microfiche displaying photographic reproductions of the newspapers from June 1973. After about an hour of shuffling from date to date, there it was: a small story in the *Irish Independent* dated 15 June 1973. Above the article was a photo of the victim, a fading black-and-white image of a smiling fair-haired boy wearing a smart jacket with a ribbon attached, perhaps his Communion outfit. The snapshot of the little boy, his face filled with joy, stood in terrible contrast to the words below it: 'BOY (7) IS FOUND DEAD.' The lurid details in the *Montreal Gazette* about 'a crude form of crucifixion' had been left out of this article, and its statement, 'it is believed the death was accidental', placed doubt even on the possibility of murder.

Next stop was the National Archives, where records of coroner's court hearings are kept. A death such as this would surely have been the subject of an inquest – open court hearings that are a matter of public record. It took a week to find the file, and when it arrived it was disappointingly thin. Its contents, however, left no doubt: the newspaper report in the *Irish Independent* had to be immediately cast aside. This death was most definitely not an accident.

It had really happened: a little boy had been murdered in Dublin in the '70s, his life taken by a teenager in what looked like a deeply disturbing ritual killing. Yet a more detailed newspaper search revealed little else. For the unfortunate boy's family, this must have been a tragedy beyond words. For Ireland and for people with an interest in criminal pathology, in our extreme acts, in the culture of the past, this was a forgotten killing, a tragedy lost to our consciousness, to our national discussion, to analysis and understanding.

# ONE

## The Boy in the Attic

In truth there were two boys in the attic. The teenager was murmuring in English, Irish and Latin while the younger boy's body hung from the rafters.

The date was 14 June 1973 and it should have been an ordinary Thursday in the quiet County Dublin village of Palmerstown. Though there was a bright and cloudless sky, near gale force winds buffeted men, tore leaves from trees, and made the day unseasonably cold. Such weather, though, is unexceptional: summer in Ireland has no guarantee of warmth, and a fine day is any day it doesn't rain.

Mr Terence Horgan had risen early, as was his habit. A businessman, he was – and still is – a devout Catholic, and that morning, as was his routine, he attended the early 7.30 a.m. Mass at nearby St Philomena's Roman Catholic Church. Before he left, he looked in on his seven-year-old son, John, who was still sleeping.

The early Mass would not have been busy. Parish curate and part-time playwright, Father Cornelius O'Keeffe (Con to his friends), conducted the Mass without undue delay, knowing that most of the men present were taking Communion before going to work. Though the world was changing, in the village of Palmerstown in the early '70s, tradition still held strong: Irish men were the family breadwinners and women had roles as housewives.

It was just a routine Thursday for Terence Horgan's wife, Anne, preparing that morning, as she did every day, breakfast for their son, John. The sandy-haired boy was loved and treasured by the entire Horgan clan, not only because he was an engaging, lively, loving little lad but also because he was Terence and Anne's only child, born just a year into their marriage, in 1965. Their wedding at St Brigid's Church in the scenic village of Hacketstown, Carlow, took place on 6 June 1964, a day when company director, Terence, and Anne, a secretary, vowed to love and honour each other till death do them part.

After their marriage the Horgans moved to number six Hollyville, a large semi-detached house on the edge of Palmerstown village. Palmerstown was popular among commuters as a rural refuge from the city yet close enough to work in the capital. Hollyville, a row of nine fine houses constructed by local builder Frank Towey, was more upmarket than most of the housing in the area. Ireland was slowly becoming more prosperous and the numbers of professionals such as civil servants, bank officials and business people were on the rise. Hollyville quickly became a small community: there were the Coffeys in number one, the McGraths in number three, up to the Boylan family in the end house, number nine. Somewhat to the bafflement of outsiders, a second row of houses, also named Hollyville, constructed by a different builder who lived close by, was also numbered one to nine. No doubt the residents were amused at the difficulties faced by visitors but, as everyone knew everyone else by name, to the locals – and, mercifully, to the postman, who knew his area well – it all made perfect sense.

A little over a year after moving into number six, the Horgans' joy was made complete by the birth in Dublin's Mount Carmel Hospital of a son, John Joseph, on 27 August 1965. He was baptised five days later in a ceremony presided over by his uncle, Redemptorist priest Father Seán Horgan, held in St Philomena's Church, just a stone's throw from their family home.

On the other side of the dividing wall of the Horgans' semi-detached house was number seven Hollyville, home to the Bales, a family who some considered to be aloof – academics who had little time for neighbourly gossip. Kenneth Bale was a civil servant attached to the Ordnance Survey in Dublin. A fluent and passionate Irish speaker, he specialised in the history of Irish place names and had even written an obscure book on the subject. Small, slightly portly, clean-shaven and with thick-rimmed glasses, Kenneth Bale was painfully shy, but this did not stop him from being a man of strong conviction and firmly held views. Fiercely right wing, he was a member of the Irish Language section of the Legion of Mary, an association of Catholic laity who brought their faith to the destitute. He was a vigorous letter writer to newspaper editors on such thorny topical issues as contraception, abortion, divorce – all outlawed in '70s Ireland – and what he saw as the general decline in public morals. Kenneth's wife, Catherine, is remembered as a quiet and retiring woman who lived modestly and was devoted to her family. Five years into their marriage their first child was born: a son, Lorcan. He was followed by a daughter, Anna, a second son, Déaglán, another daughter, Máire Eithne, and finally by their youngest girl, Cáitnona.

Number seven was semi-detached and large for the time. It needed to be. It was home not only to Mr and Mrs Bale and their five children, but also to Mrs Bale's parents, Richard and Ann Breslin. The language of the house was Irish, which was unusual for the time and place. In Ireland today the language has undergone a major revival: there are many Irish-language schools; there is the dedicated television channel TG4; there are newspapers written wholly in Irish; and a nationwide Irish-language radio station, Raidió na Gaeltachta. Most Irish people today speak at least a little of the language – this level of fluency is known locally as the '*cúpla focail*' or 'the couple of words' – and the language is now a source of great national pride. But in the '70s, although interest in the language was starting to revive, it was still not widely spoken: according to the 1971 census, 71.7 per cent of citizens spoke no Irish at all and of those who did, not that many would have used it day-to-day. It would have been somewhat unusual to find an Irish-speaking family such as the Bales in the suburbs of Dublin. The few that there were tended to be highly enthusiastic about the tongue, were often opposed to the spread of English influences in Ireland and, as in the case of Mr Bale, some were deeply conservative on moral issues.

On that cool day, 14 June 1973, the Bale family's routine was somewhat out of kilter. In preceding weeks, Mrs Bale, who had been suffering from severe cramps for several months, had heeded her doctors' advice and sought a hysterectomy. This is debilitating surgery even today, but 30 years ago it was even more demanding. Luckily the operation went well and on 14 June Mrs Bale was beginning her recovery in Dublin's Bon Secours Hospital, an institution that for the previous 20 years had provided medical facilities under the ministry of a group of nuns.

Unused to fending for themselves, Kenneth and the Bale children rustled together a simple breakfast before heading their separate ways. Kenneth Bale's views on education were as strong as his views on any other topic. He felt the mainstream education system was unsuitable for his children due to the pernicious influence of the English language. As a result, the Bale children received their education through the medium of Irish. The eldest son, Lorcan, attended Coláiste Mhuire, a school for boys set up in 1931 and managed by the Christian Brothers. The school moved to Rataoth Road on the outskirts of the city in 2003, but in 1973 it was based in Parnell Square, just off Dublin's main thoroughfare, O'Connell Street.

That summer Lorcan was sitting his Intermediate Certificate exams, taken by all Irish students at around age 16 and an important educational milestone. On the morning of 14 June, students across the country were sitting their geography paper. Lorcan was stressed: geography was one of his weakest subjects and his revision had been far from thorough. Kenneth Bale had gone so far as to install a shed in the back garden of his home where he would individually tutor his children in preparation for their upcoming exams. Clearly Mr Bale cared deeply about his children's academic success. Lorcan understood that his parents expected him to do well, but deep down he knew that his was an academically hopeless case. Worse still, his extended family were all aware that he was sitting exams because a photographer from a national paper had turned up at his school that same week to capture a select group of Irish youngsters on the first day of the Intermediate Certificate. Of the hundreds of schools in the country, the newspaper had to choose his. And of the dozens of pupils sitting their exams, Lorcan Bale's was the face pictured studiously answering the questions.

For Lorcan, the pressures were great, but success in the Intermediate Certificate would need a miracle. While he did not believe in traditional divine intervention, the boy had his own highly unconventional set of beliefs, and perhaps he felt these might ensure the results he so desperately needed.

It only took a few short hours. By lunchtime the exam was over, the words on the page could not be altered, and Lorcan must have been wondering how best to explain to his father that his chances of achieving the expected honours grade were negligible.

Arriving at his home in Palmerstown, Lorcan opened the door with his key and spoke briefly to his grandmother, Ann Breslin, and his sister, Anna. The two siblings did not get along particularly well, despite being the closest in age, only eighteen months apart. They had little in common. Lorcan was a loner, an angry teenager with few real friends. Anna despised his taste in music, which ranged from glam rock to heavy metal. That afternoon Anna and her sisters, Máire Eithne and Cáitnona, were preparing for their regular music lesson nearby. Lorcan made himself a cup of coffee and went upstairs. A pale, thin, asthmatic boy, he looked younger than his 16 years; yet for all his frail outward appearance, he was physically fit and skilled with his fists. Those who underestimated him quickly learned their mistake – Lorcan seldom lost a fight.

Lorcan lay on his bed, alone in the room he shared with his

13-year-old brother, Déaglán. It was a bright bedroom, and tidy, with books piled up in stacks. That day he was casually dressed in classic '70s bold colours: a yellow wide-collared shirt topped by a green V-necked jumper over blue trousers and white canvas shoes. Pupils past their third year at Coláiste Mhuire were not required to wear uniform and so smart casual was the norm, though Lorcan's outfits were more garish than his classmates'. As he lay on his bed, the teenager was deep in thought. Today was a day he had been anticipating for a long time. Nothing could be left to chance.

Some months earlier, Parish Curate Father Con O'Keeffe had risen early on a spring morning to prepare for the 7.30 Mass at St Philomena's Catholic Church in Palmerstown. As was the case across Ireland, daily attendances were dwindling, a great source of concern to the Church, and to Father O'Keeffe personally. However he knew he could depend on his regular flock of daily communicants, which included Mr Horgan.

Sunday Masses, at least, could be relied upon to turn out a full house. Father O'Keeffe took the spiritual welfare of his attendees very seriously. Those he called 'lurkers' – people who lingered in the entrance porch in order to make a quick getaway after Mass – obviously needed his teachings more than most, and Father O'Keeffe would make sure to herd them into the church proper, lest they miss out on any of his fiery sermons. A highly educated Irish speaker from Kerry, Father O'Keeffe was well respected, and known for his pulpit oratory, but his was no liberal message of live and let live – his voice thundered on the dangers of sin, the fires of hell, and the temptations of the devil; for the believer, he spoke of the path to redemption. This was unusual for a Catholic priest; such fire-and-brimstone messages are more characteristic of the low churches, and evangelical Protestantism.

That late spring morning, as he passed the shrine to the Virgin Mary overlooking the murky fish-pond, nothing seemed out of the ordinary. The priest unlocked the front door and entered the porch. The vials of holy water were untouched, as were the notices advocating the conservative group for laity, the Legion of Mary. And yet the cleric sensed immediately that something was wrong.

Inside the church, past the twin confessionals, Father O'Keeffe could see that the side door to the sacristy was ajar. Dread filled him. There had been rare burglaries in other churches in recent years but this was a loyal parish, one where neighbour looked after neighbour and where crime was mercifully rare. Surely it couldn't be. Stepping forward, eyes adjusting to the gloom, he saw what had been done to his church.

The sight that met him visibly weakened the priest. The high gilt crucifix, normally the centrepiece of the altar, had been moved – it now lay upside down, in a deliberate and profane mockery, with the head of Jesus pointing to the earth. The altar appeared dishevelled, but it was only when he drew closer to the tabernacle that the true extent of the desecration became clear. The small wooden door of the tabernacle box was ajar, and Father O'Keeffe could now see what had been taken. The silver Communion chalice was missing – but worse, so were three holy Eucharist wafers. The very host itself – that when consecrated would become the *actual Body of Christ* – had been stolen.

In recent years there have been some high-profile cases involving the theft or desecration of the Eucharist, such as American student Webster Cook, who took Communion but later removed the wafer from his mouth and placed it in a clear plastic bag, which he refused to return until granted a meeting with the local bishop. It was a deeply divisive act – Catholics worldwide decried the appalling mockery and desecration of the very body of Christ, while many others who did not share the faith still saw it as deeply disrespectful. However others found it amusing, or puzzling, that there could be such outrage over the treatment of what they saw as nothing more than a cracker. But Cook's stunt occurred in 2008 in America; in Ireland in 1973 such a thing would have been utterly unimaginable.

Horrified, the priest hurried to set things to rights before any of the faithful arrived. If anyone noticed his sermon that morning was unusually rushed, they said nothing. But in the weeks ahead he would consider how best to react to this appalling violation. Already, he was considering the right form of words to announce to the next Sunday's congregation that persons unknown had stolen the Communion chalice, and the words to appeal for its safe return.

Getting up from the bed, Lorcan Bale moved to the wardrobe and started removing the clothes hung on their hangers within, laying them across his brother's bed. This allowed him to step into the wardrobe unhindered. Reaching as high as he could, the boy was able to touch the ceiling of the wardrobe, and pushing on one 18-inch square section revealed something no one else in the Bale household knew of: a trapdoor. It hid a rope and pulley, which allowed the opening of a second trapdoor above the first. A casual visitor to Lorcan's bedroom – and there were very few – would completely miss this construction, which must have taken several months to build. Lorcan had been careful to keep his secret: his parents certainly did not know of it, and even his 13-year-old brother, with whom he shared the bedroom, was unaware of the concealed entrance to the roof space.

With the ease of months of practice, Lorcan climbed up, through both trapdoors, and into the unlit space of the attic beyond. At one end were boxes of old books, heirlooms and the hand-me-downs common to many a roof space of the time. And at the other end from where Lorcan stood was a raised rostrum, upon which you could just about make out a number of items lit by a tiny shaft of summer sunshine sneaking into the attic. Carefully manipulating himself closer to the rostrum, Lorcan fumbled for a box of Friendly matches (instantly recognisable by their pink tip, these were the forerunner of the modern safety match and their selling point was that they could be struck on any rough surface). After running the match along an upright rafter, the flame burned just long enough for Lorcan to light two candles wedged in homemade holders placed on the rostrum. He lit a Churchman's cigarette. As the candlelight illuminated the scene, the boy surveyed the items in front of him: several saucers brimming with white powders; a plastic container holding human faeces; a communion wafer (the platform of the Catholic Mass); and, the centrepiece, a shiny silver chalice – the very same one stolen from St Philomena's Church weeks previously. It was the boy's most prized possession. But there was one more offering to make. Lorcan pulled his thin body toward the far end of the attic where a rug was covering another stolen item. Pulling back the blanket, he manoeuvred its bulky metal form so that it rested close to the altar.

It was a child's small Raleigh Chipper bicycle.

John Horgan would have been excited leaving Mount Sackville Convent School on the edge of Dublin's Phoenix Park that Thursday afternoon. The previous weeks had been happy ones for the family; aside from visiting friends and relations, including the boy's aunt who lived in one of Dublin's coastal suburbs, John Horgan had just a few short weeks earlier celebrated his First Holy Communion, a rite of passage where he received his first Sacrament of the Holy Eucharist – a milestone in his young life, a cause for celebration for John and his large extended family. The summer holidays were just days away: over two long, carefree months stretching ahead. Traditionally, Irish children have received more generous summer holidays than their UK counterparts, because in an historically agricultural nation every pair of hands was needed to help with the harvest. But farming was very far from the seven year old's mind that day. His mother had chosen to visit the recuperating Mrs Bale in hospital and John was to spend the afternoon in the care of the Bale family. Before leaving for the hospital in Glasnevin, Mrs Horgan lifted John over the low wall separating the Horgan and Bale back gardens, handing her son over to the kindly Bale grandmother, Mrs Ann Breslin.

There is no record of how young John would have felt being

left in the care of the Bale family, but we do know that they were close neighbours, always willing to help each other out when needed. A curious, inquisitive boy, John was fascinated by the pet canary owned by the Bales. Shortly after his mother lifted him over the back wall that afternoon, Mrs Breslin carried the canary, which was in its cage, to the back garden, where John sat and watched the little bird. Mrs Breslin told him that the three Bale girls were all at music lessons, but that he could play with them as soon as they returned home. John was well used to amusing himself. There were not many children of his age living in Hollyville at that time – friends recall John as a likeable small boy who would watch the bigger boys playing football from the sidelines in the field behind Hollyville. The older boys did not deliberately exclude John from their games, it was simply that he was too young to cope with the rough and tumble of boisterous teenagers.

While little John's preoccupation that day never went further than innocent curiosity about the well-being of the Bales' caged canary, Lorcan Bale's mind was in an altogether darker place. He had been interested in the occult for many years, an interest that had descended into an obsession; now his fascination had reached a new and chilling level. For several months he had been hurting, then later killing, animals – mainly rats but also dogs, cats and pet mice. But he had decided, in what must have seemed to him like a logical progression, that animals were no longer good enough. His needs and creed demanded something new – the sacrifice of a human child. This was not a spur of the moment decision; Lorcan had considered the idea for some time, moulding and fashioning his murderous thoughts until every detail had been perfected. As he lay on his bed early that Thursday afternoon, the teenager had already decided that today was the day he would finally carry out his plan.

Later Lorcan would confess to authorities,

I had a cup of coffee and I went to my room. I rested there

for about an hour. While I was there I was considering getting John, that is John Horgan, the seven-year-old boy who lives next door. I planned how I would do it, meaning how I would kill him and hide his body. I then started getting things I needed to carry out my plan. I got the club. Then I went down to the tool shed and I got a sack and as much rope as I could find. I also brought down neck ties from my room when I was going to the tool shed.

Quite casually, Lorcan Bale entered the back garden of his house where John was still engrossed with the captive canary. Keeping an eye on the boy on that June afternoon was Lorcan's grandfather, Richard Breslin. The teenager sidled up to the seven year old and asked him if he would like to look for rabbits in the field behind the house. All the children in Hollyville were quite familiar with the back field – it was their shared playground, accessed from the rear garden of every house. John eagerly agreed and moments later the pair had climbed the low fence into the large meadow that straddled the nine houses. In Lorcan's pockets were the club, the rope and the neck ties, while the sack was tightly rolled up in his hand. As the two boys strolled across the meadow on that bright June afternoon, only Lorcan knew that his plan was now in motion, like a train with its own unstoppable momentum. Today the field is bisected by the busy N4 dual carriageway linking Dublin with Galway, but in 1973 it was an altogether more tranquil spot. Tortoiseshell butterflies, flowering yellow bracken, thistles, a stream – and, of course, rabbits.

Like any little boy, John was curious about the world around him, and the chance to look for rabbits in the back field was an opportunity he was not going to miss. The pair walked in the sunshine and settled at a hedge, a position only Lorcan knew had been carefully chosen to be out of sight of the houses. Having already caught rats in this area weeks earlier, he was able to point out to the younger boy a rat hole in the undergrowth. Lorcan gestured towards the burrow, telling the younger boy that here was a burrow where he might possibly actually glimpse an elusive rabbit. John crouched down to peer into the undergrowth, and at that moment Lorcan Bale placed the sack on the grass and pulled from his pocket the wooden club.

The police report written the next day by a Sergeant Patrick McGirr in a letter to Dr Bartley Sheehan, Dublin County Coroner, reads, 'Lorcan Bale invited the child out into a field behind his house to look for rabbits. He clubbed the deceased from behind as he was looking at a rabbit hole, which he, Bale, had pointed out to him.' The only mercy in this vicious act was that John could not have seen or felt the impending attack, and when it came, according to the autopsy report, his brain injuries were so severe that death would have swiftly followed the blow. In short, John Horgan's life was cruelly extinguished, but it is unlikely he ever felt any pain.

Lorcan Bale paused, staring at the little body crumpled at his feet. A minute ago, he had been a teenage loner. Now he was a murderer. John's body lay next to the rat hole and, apart from the swelling on the back of his head, he had no visible injuries. Very carefully, Lorcan began to tie up the lifeless little boy's hands and legs and, perhaps believing the boy to be only unconscious, he placed a gag in his mouth. Then he heaved the body into the brown canvas sack, and tied the top of it with his school tie. Walking casually, as though enjoying the fine June day, he strolled back towards his house carrying the sack. About 100 yards from the murder spot, Lorcan saw two boys approaching. He quickly put the sack in a hedge and covered it with nettles. The boys, Michael Smallwood and Damian Dempster, both aged 12, walked towards Bale; they had no reason to believe he was not the only other person in the field. But Lorcan did not want the boys to approach too closely and gestured to them to go away. Later one boy would tell police that Lorcan Bale had made a 'rude sign with his fingers'. The other spoke about the teenager giving them 'the V-sign'. This gesture coming from a boy four years older than them was enough to make the pair withdraw. Lorcan stood his ground, staying alongside the hedge until Dempster and

Smallwood were both completely out of sight, at which point he repositioned the body, more carefully concealed this time, in another hedge.

The murder of John Horgan was only the first phase of Lorcan Bale's evil plan. It was shortly after 4.30 in the afternoon when the teenager walked home to retrieve a rucksack. With chilling calmness he fetched a haversack, a grey camping backpack with brown leather straps, and returned to the spot where he had concealed the body. However he had difficulty placing the body inside the rucksack. John Horgan was half an inch above four feet tall – average height for a healthy seven year old – and the haversack proved unfit for the grim purpose of holding him. But by tying the shoulder strap to the front of the rucksack and placing the other strap across his back, Bale was able to conceal the body and begin to haul it towards the gate that led to the main road. Suddenly he was startled by the arrival in the field of another unwelcome visitor, this time a local boy, Colin Nolan. This boy would later report that Lorcan Bale was both panting and smiling. Colin was curious as to why the teenager was struggling with a heavy backpack, hardly a routine sight at any time. He asked Lorcan Bale if he was carrying coal in the rucksack. Bale, irritated by yet another interruption to his plan and clearly not wanting to engage in conversation, stated that he was. Satisfied with his explanation, the young Nolan boy continued on his way.

Lorcan Bale left the field by the gate that connected to the main road and when he had almost reached his home was stopped by two brothers playing in their front garden. They too were curious as to the contents of the sack. Bale's reply this time was that he had been collecting firewood for a barbecue that his parents were planning. Moments later he was home, at number seven Hollyville. There he placed the haversack containing the child's body in the garage and went into the house.

Around half an hour had passed since John Horgan's life had been so suddenly cut short. Lorcan Bale peered into the kitchen where Mr Bale, grandmother Ann Breslin, his brother Déaglán and sister Anna were having their dinner. Without entering the kitchen, he closed the door into the hallway and walked upstairs. Once safely in his bedroom, he climbed up through the wardrobe into the attic and began to make preparations for the moment he had so meticulously planned. In the roof space, he had constructed an elaborate shrine, adding elements piece by piece over the previous year. After lighting a number of candles, Bale returned to the garden, retrieved the body from the garage and silently carried it upstairs, anxious not to disturb his family while they were finishing their evening meal. Carefully placing the boy's remains on his bed, the teenager went downstairs once again and retrieved a ladder stored in the back garden. He tiptoed upstairs and leaned the ladder against the entrance to the homemade trapdoor.

Holding the lifeless figure once encased in the sack, Lorcan Bale inched his way into the roof space, a process which resulted in some bruising to the dead boy's body. Coroner Professor Maurice Hickey would later note in his report that, 'multiple bruises were present on the backs of both shoulders and there were multiple small bruises on the fronts of both shins,' injuries consistent with the manhandling of the body into the confined roof space. Professor Hickey added that, aside from the head wound, 'there were no other external marks of injury anywhere else on the body'.

The evidence of what actually occurred in the attic that day is incomplete. Through surviving documentation and interviews with those who were present, we can achieve a clear picture of what happened in the roof space – though the question of why the shocking events happened can only be answered by one person: Lorcan Bale. It is known that the boy's body was first removed from the sack and laid down on the joists. The teenager checked the boy's heartbeat to see if there were any signs of life. There were none. Loosening the ropes that were around the hands, the teenage murderer took a thick red rope previously placed in the attic and tied the body to a vertical beam that ran from the roof to the attic floor. With the abdomen and feet secure in an apparent standing position, he tied the hands outstretched. He paused, observing for some minutes the motionless form before him spread-eagled in a cruciform posture. Satisfied with his handiwork, he blew out all but two of the candles and went downstairs.

While the events of that afternoon are beyond question, what is far more difficult to reveal is the exact motivation behind this bizarre ritual. That Lorcan Bale believed himself to be a satanist is not in any doubt. Present were all the elements he considered necessary for a black mass: the candles, faeces, the Host, the Communion chalice and, overseeing it all, the body of a pure innocent child. In its simplest form the black mass is a mockery of the Catholic Mass; its main objective is the profanation of the Host. Contemporary writings may have influenced Bale, the most notable being Anton LaVey's 1969 work, *The Satanic Bible*. But how this teenager born into a devoutly Catholic Irish family was able to descend so deeply into the darkest reaches of the occult is a question requiring a great deal of thought, and one this book must attempt to answer.

Were these the actions of a lonely teenager hopelessly immersed in the occult? Was there a sexual motive? Was he simply jealous of John, a much-loved only child of caring parents? Or was Lorcan Bale a victim of a higher darker power; was he in a mental place where he was way past the boundaries of rational thought and therefore not of sound mind? These questions were to be addressed in the months ahead by law enforcement authorities, medical investigators, religious clerics and by the families of those touched by this shocking murder. But on that Thursday afternoon, the tiny community of Hollyville was about to learn of a darkness in their midst, a stain which would haunt this little village for decades to come.

In the kitchen, Lorcan made a cup of tea for himself and as he was drinking, his grandmother, Mrs Breslin, walked into the room. After initially enquiring about how Lorcan had fared in his geography exam earlier that day, she began to ask about John Horgan, whom she had not seen since Lorcan had taken him from the back garden to search for rabbits about an hour previously. Quickly her concern mounted. In a few short minutes her demeanour changed from gentle curiosity to acute nervousness and increasing worry. The teenager's reply was that John must be still out in the fields and was likely playing with other neighbouring children.

News travelled quickly in that tiny tight-knit community that the Horgan boy was missing and within minutes the Bale house was filled with worried Hollyville residents who quickly set about searching for the seven year old, calling his name at the top of their voices. Lorcan, too, chose to join in the search, seizing on a friend, Kieran McAllister, who had called to the house, and asking him to help look for John. With chilling calmness, the young killer went through the charade of searching for the missing boy. He knew that he was displaying outward concern while at the same time hiding the murderous truth. The pair were joined by Lorcan's sister Anna, who by then had returned from music lessons, as well as Anna's friend from number eight Hollyville, Leilah Nolan. The crowd swelled; one neighbour, Mrs Sweeney from number four, asked Lorcan directly if he knew what had happened to John Horgan. Another volunteer searcher, Joe Doyle, recalls the mounting concern for the little boy's well-being:

> We began by searching fields and ditches, particularly in the big field behind Hollyville. That was where John was last seen and that was where all the kids used to play.
>
> Today Hollyville is a quiet cul-de-sac, but then it was on the main Dublin to Galway highway. The late afternoon rush hour would see a doubling in the volume of cars, commuter buses and lorries. But there were other equally deadly dangers. Across the road, behind Maxie Cosgrove's stud farm, flowed the River Liffey, barely 500 yards as the

crow flies from Hollyville. So our biggest fear was that he
had wandered off in that direction and been swept away in
the fast flowing river.

However the searchers at that stage never considered that the
Horgan boy had been the victim of sinister circumstances. 'To
us,' recalled Doyle, 'there were just three options: either John
had wandered off and had got lost, in which case we would surely
find him; or that he had somehow slipped and fallen in the
hedgerows; or, Heaven forbid, in the worst case, that he had
perished in a tragic accident. We just didn't consider any other
possibilities.'

Another searcher was local butcher Dessie Cloak who, with his
wife and three daughters, lived around 50 yards from the Horgans.
He knew the family well; young John would have been an
occasional visitor to the house, as indeed was Lorcan Bale. His
own concern was a building site at the farthest end of the field
behind Hollyville, where foundations were being dug for new
houses by machinery that stood idle and largely unprotected.
Could the young boy have somehow injured himself at this
construction site? A thorough search yielded nothing and the
men continued looking for the child, calling his name and
combing the hedgerows.

As the hunt became ever more intense, Lorcan Bale slipped
away from the search and returned to his home. Collecting a pair
of scissors from the kitchen, he went to his bedroom, ascended to
the attic and once again lit candles so that he could properly
observe his grim enterprise. Very carefully, yet inexplicably, he
used the scissors to cut off John's clothes until before him in the
half light was the pale, naked body of the boy, suspended vertically
from the rafters, legs together, arms outstretched, in a depraved,
grotesque parody of the crucifixion. One can barely imagine what
must have been passing through the mind of Lorcan Bale.

The timeline of the day's events reveals a gap when the
whereabouts and activities of Lorcan Bale are unknown. He
returned from school around midday, rested and began making

preparations for the murder. It is believed that John Horgan died instantly in the attack that took place around 4 p.m. Half an hour later the teenager had brought the body back to his house and by 5 p.m. he had hauled the boy's remains upstairs. His grandmother, Ann Breslin, was the first to note John's absence at what cannot have been later than 6 p.m., more likely some minutes before the hour. The search began immediately and we know that Ann Breslin left to visit her daughter, Mrs Catherine Bale, in Dublin's Bon Secours Hospital at 7 p.m. The missing boy's father returned from work around 8 p.m., having spent the day with business clients in the country. This leaves a one-hour period between 7 p.m. and 8 p.m. when there is no written account, nor any witness testimony stating where Lorcan Bale was or what he was doing.

With the return of Mr Horgan at 8 p.m., the search further escalated. A highly respected and well-liked businessman, Terence Horgan must have been worried beyond words yet he showed few outward signs of panic. He quickly established that the last person to have seen his son alive was the lanky 16 year old from next door. Lorcan's younger brother, Déaglán, was in the Horgan house, and Mr Horgan told him to find his brother because he wanted to speak to him at once. Déaglán relayed the message and moments later Mr Horgan and Lorcan Bale faced each other across the low wall that separated the two neighbouring gardens. One witness who was a child at the time recalls Mr Horgan grabbing the teenager by the throat before shouting, 'Where's my son? Where's my son?' Another account differs, stating that they had a very direct conversation at the garden wall in which Lorcan told Mr Horgan that during the afternoon he had gone to the field to study for his upcoming exams and John had gone with him. The teenager's best explanation for the boy's absence was that while he had been immersed in a textbook, John had wandered off and had not been seen since. Mr Horgan asked Lorcan Bale to show him the exact spot where he had taken his son and so the pair walked purposefully into the field where Bale pointed to a grassy corner and said that this was where he had last seen the child.

At one point after this, Lorcan Bale was seen by his brother watching the family's black-and-white television. The programme was the American detective series *Ironside*, about a wheelchair-bound cop who would solve a myriad of crimes each week. According to the TV listings for that night, *Ironside* was broadcast on Irish state channel RTÉ between 9 p.m. and 10 p.m., at a time when the search for the Horgan boy was intensifying with the evening light beginning to fade. Ironically the episode was titled 'If a Body See a Body' – 'a corpse disappears and Sgt Brown has only a precocious youngster to prove that it ever existed'.

The children of Hollyville joined in the search, but were largely unaware of the true nature of the tragedy that was unfolding. While the older boys and girls combed the fields calling the name of the missing child, the younger children congregated at the entrance to the estate, watching the events unfold. Later that evening, when the police became involved, the younger children were told to go inside, that the search was over. Eventually some were told that the Horgan boy had died and that they would in the coming days attend his funeral but, from that moment on, the circumstances of his death became a taboo, unspoken subject. What happened in Hollyville stayed in Hollyville.

The police telephone log at Lucan Garda station for that evening reads, 'at 9.3pm (*sic*) Terence Horgan of 6 Hollyville, reported to the Gardaí at Lucan that his son was missing from home'. The police response was swift and within minutes the civilian searchers were joined by men in uniform backed up by sniffer dogs. Leading the team was Detective Inspector Willie Reynolds, who would take overall responsibility for the case. His right-hand man, Detective Sergeant Jim Noonan, would become the law enforcement officer most actively involved in the investigation. Detective Sergeant Noonan would be heavily immersed in the decision-making process, and later would take possession of most of the exhibits, as well as interviewing most of the witnesses and the one suspect.

With local officers already searching the area, the squad car carrying Noonan and Reynolds arrived in Hollyville at 10.20 p.m. that evening, the pair having heard that concerns were mounting for the missing seven-year-old boy. There to meet them was a local police officer, Detective Garda Terence Smyth, based at Lucan station some five miles from Hollyville. The young detective was in the field behind the Hollyville houses, talking to Lorcan Bale and his father, Kenneth. Casually dressed in a khaki jacket to keep himself warm on that chilly June evening, Lorcan confirmed to the men in uniform that he was the last to see John Horgan, and repeated his story about John having wandered off while he had been engrossed in a study book. The young killer's lies continued, adding that the final glimpse he had of John Horgan was seeing the little boy walking in the direction of the Hollyville houses.

Almost four decades later I tracked down Jim Noonan, now living in retirement following a distinguished lifetime of service with An Garda Síochána, Ireland's national police force. Five years after the murder of John Horgan, Noonan was promoted to the rank of detective inspector where he served for twelve years in a south-Dublin district. Later he rose to the rank of superintendent where, at Garda headquarters in Phoenix Park, he took on responsibility for the building of several new, purpose-built police stations, professional units constructed specifically for the needs of a modern police force. Finding Jim Noonan was something of a breakthrough: many of those involved in the 1973 investigation had passed on and he was one of a handful of professional witnesses with clear recollections of the events of that June day. We agreed to meet at a hotel in the shadow of Kilmainham Jail, a place of pilgrimage for Irish people as it was here that many of the heroes of the 1916 Easter Rising were executed by British forces. Noonan was returning from a funeral and we found each other easily, quickly seeking refuge in a quiet corner away from a boisterous group of American tourists. Tall, grey and distinguished, Jim Noonan had investigated numerous murders in his long career, but this one was different. He declined the offer of a cup of tea or anything stronger and quickly addressed the business in hand.

'When a young child goes missing, you would be concerned straight away, particularly if the child has been gone for more than two hours. The normal procedure is to launch immediate searches, talk to friends, family and to neighbours. It's also critical to find and interview the last person known to have seen the child alive.'

'So when you arrived at the scene and established that a teenage neighbour, Lorcan Bale, was the last person seen with the boy, how did you approach him?' I asked.

The retired Detective paused, considering carefully his response. 'You have to approach the matter with an open yet inquisitive mind. You listen to and assess a person's answers but also look at their demeanour. Lorcan Bale was quite cool given the circumstances, but he was also quite shifty and seemed to show signs of nervousness.'

Noonan was choosing his words cautiously. A lifetime of policing had taught him never to be careless with language. His answers were open, honest and precise, so it was important that my questions had matching precision.

'Your immediate priority was clearly the search for the missing boy and that search was ongoing at the time that you spoke to Lorcan Bale. But at what point in your own mind did the teenager change from being a witness to being a suspect?'

This was a question that Noonan had no trouble in addressing. 'I recall Lorcan Bale telling me that he had seen the boy crossing the main road and entering the field at a gate that leads to the River Liffey – this was at the front of the house, not the field at the back of the house where it turned out that the murder took place.' He added, 'We were standing on the pavement next to the main road. I asked him to show me exactly where he was standing when he saw the Horgan boy crossing the road. We walked the few yards to the spot and looked across the main road, but from that position you couldn't see the gate where Lorcan Bale claimed that he had last seen John Horgan. That was the moment when I knew something was amiss.'

On that June evening in 1973, Detective Sergeant Jim Noonan was less than impressed by Lorcan Bale's account and discreetly pulled the teenager's father to one side. Mr Bale confessed that his son had had behavioural issues of late, that he was hostile towards his family and particularly towards his sisters. He added that as his father he had tried to reason with the boy, but that Lorcan had questioned his father's values, even the validity of his Catholic faith.

Digesting this information, the detective and Mr Bale returned to the spot in the back field where Lorcan Bale was now standing. The teenager's father raised his voice, pleading with his son to tell whatever he knew, saying that a young child was missing and that this was not a time to hold back a single morsel of information, no matter how small the detail. Detective Sergeant Noonan weighed in with his own appeal, 'Listen to me very carefully. If there's an accident, there's a chance that John Horgan may be still alive, and if we get to him in time, we may be able to save him.' For the first time that day, Lorcan Bale appeared visibly uneasy. Noonan observed that the boy's hands were making a continuous motion, alternately wringing his fingers and pulling at the sleeves of his khaki jacket.

Watching this exchange, another officer, Detective Whyte, spoke: 'We'll search the house.'

Detective Inspector Willie Reynolds added, 'We'll search the house from top to bottom.'

As the last light faded from the June sky, Lorcan Bale looked at the three uniformed men and then to his father. Lowering his head, he whispered, 'I'll show you.'

'Where is he?' asked Detective Sergeant Noonan, softly.

'In the attic.'

# Two

## Love thy Neighbour

Palmerstown today is a suburban district west of Dublin, connected to the city by a busy motorway. While it has its scenic spots, it is in most ways unremarkable. Turning off the main road we find a short stretch of shops: a general store, a bank, a busy bookmakers, a discount sofa warehouse, three takeaways and, at the end of the road, a nice flower shop next to a busy pub. Largely residential, the area is quiet in the daytime, with homeowners mostly at work and children at school.

Despite its modest size, the village has a history going back almost a thousand years, and the origin of its name remains unclear. It may be connected with Ireland's first hospital, the Hospital of St John the Baptist, founded around 1180 by Aelred, known as 'The Dane', a pilgrim or 'palmer' who had visited the Holy Land. At the time, pilgrims wore palm leaves on their lapels and so were known as 'palmers'. By the eighteenth century the village had gained notoriety for its summer horse and cattle fair, which was famed for drunkenness, fighting, thieving, roguery and general bad behaviour. One of the more notable incidents at Palmerstown fair occurred in August 1738. A rowdy young nobleman, the fourth Lord Santry, became argumentative with other drinkers and twice attempted to draw his sword but, being so inebriated, failed on both occasions and stormed out in temper. He shouted that he would kill the next man who uttered a word. A local porter, Loughlin Murphy, spoke up, and within seconds he was lying on the ground in a pool of blood, shouting out, 'I am killed!' In fact it took a further six weeks for Murphy to die from his wounds. The following spring Lord Santry found himself facing a murder charge in the House of Lords. The evidence against his Lordship was overwhelming, and the 23 peers declared at the end of the trial that he was, 'Guilty, upon mine honour.' Under normal circumstances this verdict would have been enough to send the accused to the gallows but, perhaps due to his noble birth, the King granted Lord Santry a reprieve followed by a full pardon, although only after he was stripped of his title and banished from Ireland for life.

Ask any local for the way to Palmerstown and, being an Irish village, a pub is likely to be mentioned in the directions. One popular local landmark on the edge of town is the Deadman's Inn, which, as its name suggests, is linked with another historical demise. Back in the winter of 1798, a year of rebellion in Ireland, district judge Lord Norbury was travelling by stagecoach to his manor house in Clane, some 15 miles away. To refer to the judge as a colourful character would be an understatement: a deft combination of bribery and deception brought Norbury to the bench where he was widely regarded as corrupt and fearsome, quickly earning the name 'the Hanging Judge'. Norbury's courts were described as wild theatres: the *Dictionary of National Biography* states, 'his scanty knowledge of the law, his gross partiality, his callousness, and his buffoonery, completely disqualified him for the position. His court was in constant uproar owing to his noisy merriment. He joked even when the life of a human being was hanging in the balance.' His most famous trial was that of Irish patriot Robert Emmet. Norbury continually interrupted and abused Emmet as he was making his emotional farewell speech from the dock. The judge then donned the black cap and sentenced him to death.

With such a volatile passenger, it is not surprising that the stagecoach driver was of a nervous disposition driving west that November evening in 1798. Ignoring the fact that the judge was plainly in a hurry to get home, he slowed the stagecoach almost to a halt, intending to allow his assistant to alight and seek respite from a severe fever at a nearby coach house. The judge was furious that their speed had dropped and bellowed that he would see them both flogged and 'hanged for that matter'. The driver promptly whipped the horses to a canter. Minutes later, as the stagecoach reached Murray's Inn in Palmerstown at the greatest of speed, the carriage hit a bump in the path and the sickly assistant fell from the coach onto the bank below. The driver, fearful for his neck, drove on. The next day, the unfortunate assistant was found to have perished from exposure at the spot now known as Deadman's Inn. After a brief police investigation, the Hanging Judge was deemed to have been blameless in this sorry affair.

By the '70s Palmerstown was a popular commuter suburban village, having attracted both people from the surrounding area and families moving from the west of Ireland to seek a better livelihood in the capital. Palmerstown itself was quite typical of many Irish country hamlets where church and school were the focal points for the community. Irish people were uniformly devout; opposition to the word of the Catholic Church was negligible, indeed there seemed little reason to oppose. In Palmerstown as in many other Irish towns at the time, Sunday Mass was often standing room only, and most people sent their children to the local primary school, St Lorcan's, where the influence of the Church was both considerable and broadly welcome. Prominent past pupils of St Lorcan's include one of Ireland's most popular broadcasters, Joe Duffy, as well as Irish international footballers Jeff Kenna and Glenn Whelan.

At the edge of the village on the main Dublin-to-Lucan road stood St Philomena's Church, presided over by parish priest Father Kevin Daly and two curates Cornelius 'Con' O'Keeffe and Pat Guckian. While not the senior religious cleric in the parish, Con O'Keeffe figures prominently in the events of 1973. A fluent Irish speaker from Kerry on Ireland's Atlantic coast, he is remembered with a certain fear, but also as a man of sincerity who was well respected in the village. A fact unknown to many of his parishioners was that O'Keeffe was also an accomplished playwright, who used the pseudonym Coleman O'Shannon. When not scriptwriting for Irish television's award-winning religious affairs documentary series *Radharc*, the young curate would spend his evenings penning one-act audience participation plays, comedy dramas in which some of the actors were plants among the audience. His best-known work, *The Later Days of Cole*, went on a nationwide tour, picking up many awards along the way. During one performance in the Kerry town of Tralee, one audience member – a plant – stood up and berated an actor on stage for being a miserly father to his young daughter. The heckler became ever more vocal until his rant filled the entire auditorium. This was too much for a local Garda police officer, who shuffled his way along the aisles until he was square with the heckler. 'Get the fuck out of here,' barked the Garda, lifting the unfortunate actor by the lapels before physically manhandling him from the theatre.

Approximately 100 yards beyond St Philomena's Church was an Esso petrol station, and from it ran the straight line of houses that made up Hollyville. These houses were completely different from those of the village: larger, mostly with garages and fine rectangular gardens, they attracted middle-class, professional owners: businessmen, some of Ireland's top publicans, senior civil servants, a retired police superintendent. There was a highly charged religious mix in Hollyville: most of the men would attend Mass each day, without fail; almost every male child was an altar boy, including Lorcan Bale; there was a passing evangelical Sunday School; one local was involved in Scientology; another was a senior Irish Mormon who would host an American soul singer on his occasional forays to Ireland; many of the children were sent to retreats in the Dublin mountains organised by Marriage Encounter, then a Catholic marriage renewal programme. Religion was deeply embedded in the Hollyville community. This was very much in contrast with the more working-class houses in

Palmerstown, where property prices averaged £1,500 (in Hollyville houses cost three times that amount). While the villagers were largely devout, their religious views were generally more casual than those of their more upmarket neighbours.

Behind the Hollyville houses was a large field, bisected by a stream and a low hedge. This was more than just a place for cows to roam and rabbits to graze: 'the back field', as it was known, was the playground for all of Hollyville's children. 'It was nothing less than the centre of our lives,' one contemporary recalled. Another equated the back field with long happy days playing football, a time when the sun always shone, a time when friendships meant more than material possessions, a time when in truth nothing mattered more than who scored the winning goal. 'Occasionally someone would drag a petrol lawnmower over their wall and make a football pitch in the field, then with sweaters or sticks for goalposts, we would be good to go. It was like having our own mini Wembley in Palmerstown.' Soccer was the game of choice; the Hollyville kids seemed to show less interest in the national sports of Gaelic football or hurling. Without enough players for proper matches, the youngsters played 'three and in', where players individually aimed to score three goals and if successful would then become the goalkeeper. Scattered throughout the field were a dozen or so trees – ash, Irish oak, horse chestnut, beech – some would have been seedlings up to 100 years previously and their breadth made them ideal for climbing, a pastime almost as popular as football among the young folk of Hollyville. The very best climbing trees were just beyond the last of the houses, past a cattle pen and a cow trough, and were deemed out of bounds by most parents. Indeed, this was a street where neighbour looked after neighbour, each keeping a close eye on any child in the area. Youngsters, especially those of primary school age, were discouraged from playing at the front of the houses alongside the heavy volume of lorries and cars plying the main Dublin-to-Galway road. The constant rumble also took its toll on the structure of the houses. With double glazing not in widespread use, glass-fronted doors were known to crack as a direct result of the endless vibration from passing lorries. 'Being near the main road without a good reason got me a clip on the ear,' one man, now in his 40s, stated, his balding face beaming with a fond smile. PlayStations, the Internet and the iPod were not yet even a spark in an inventor's mind, so '70s children had to make good with the simple pleasures of the back field. Yet for almost all, their memories – apart from one terrible stain – were of an idyllic place to grow up.

John Joseph Horgan, a much-loved only child, lived all the seven years of his short life in Hollyville. He enjoyed the routine of a stable family life: the journey to school, homework, playing in the field, visiting relations and, like all of the Hollyville kids, Mass on Sunday. However, unlike most of the local children, John did not attend the primary school on the edge of the village. Instead he was enrolled in Mount Sackville School, one of Dublin's leading private schools. While the building where the boy attended classes has recently been replaced by an updated modern structure, a peer into the archives reveals that Mount Sackville has an interesting history, one where religion and education ride hand in glove. Established in 1890, the school is run by the Sisters of Saint Joseph of Cluny, an order of nuns founded by a French woman, Anne-Marie Javouhey. For her time, the nun's ideas were surprisingly radical: 'I have promised God to give myself wholly to the service of the sick and the instruction of little children,' she wrote in one of her letters to her father. Anne-Marie believed passionately that all people are equal, with a right to human and spiritual formation. Her educational methods show great respect for liberty of the human spirit: 'Free persons are led, not by constraint, but by persuasion,' she declared.

So it was within this ethos of mutual tolerance and respect that John Horgan began his schooling. Friends and neighbours recall a popular, slight, softly spoken, fair-haired boy, not at all aggressive and generally well liked. His parents kept a close eye on him, would have always known where to find him whenever he was under their supervision, and instilled in their son the importance of good manners. While the Bale family in number seven lived alongside the Horgans in the same semi-detached building, on the other side, one door down at number five Hollyville, Michael and Eilish Cully became very attached to the little boy next door. Young John would often open the front gate for Michael as he drove to work in the morning. A childless couple, in some ways John was the son they never had; they doted on the boy and he was equally fond of them. On the day he went missing, the Cullys helped in the search, and on hearing the tragic news Michael was completely devastated by grief and anger.

There were a few – not many – boys of John's age living in the street. Three doors away, the McGrath boys, Philip and Gabriel, occasionally played with young John. Six doors down from the Horgans, Eoin MacElhinney was the same age as John and the pair were friends. In '70s Ireland formalities were expected and observed. Adults would be addressed only as Mr and Mrs; a child would be welcome in another child's home but would have to wait to be invited. If a child were asked to come to a neighbour's house to watch television, the choice of viewing would have been limited. In single-channel, black-and-white Ireland, the puppet show *Wanderly Wagon* captivated the nation's young with its unfeasible plot involving a sensible dog, a gangster fox and a sarcastic crow travelling in a flying horse-drawn caravan to rescue princesses and generally do good deeds. Eoin MacElhinney has clear memories of playing football in the Horgans' large back garden where a football goal with proper nets stood at the centre of the lawn – a far cry from the sticks and sweaters in the back field. Mr Horgan would occasionally join in too, a strong, stocky, dark-haired man, clean shaven with his hair in a neat parting. A good-looking man in his 30s who often wore a trim sports jacket, he clearly enjoyed those precious moments of relaxation with his son and the boy's pals, kicking their orange football around the garden.

On one occasion John was invited for High Tea with the

MacElhinney family – Eoin, his older brother, Robert, and their parents. Before the visitor's arrival, the MacElhinney boys were told to be on their best behaviour and not to let the family down by showing poor table manners, for example by dipping bread into their fried egg. Young John Horgan arrived and took his place at the kitchen table. As the meal was placed in front of him, the boy raised his head in a manner that Oliver Twist might have done when looking for more, and politely asked: 'Mrs MacElhinney, may I have a napkin please?'

Eoin, looking puzzled, immediately demanded of his mother, 'What's a napkin?'

The question has slipped into the MacElhinney clan lore, to be repeated whenever other relations feel that Eoin – now with his own family – deserves a ribbing. It is a silly story, nothing more, but it does demonstrate that John Horgan was polite and well brought up.

Paul Browne was a few months younger than John and has fond memories of his neighbour. The Brownes lived just beyond the Esso petrol station, no more than 100 yards from the Horgan's house. One of a large family of seven children – six boys and a girl – Paul was quite similar in character to John Horgan and they became firm friends: each gentle, shy and kind, both willing to share their toys with one another. They even looked similar: slight, with fair hair and blue eyes. The Horgans would welcome young Paul into their home, a tastefully decorated house with bookshelves snaking all the way to the upstairs level. Paul remembers being offered cake and lemonade as they played in John's large Formula One-replica pedal car. In the weeks after the murder, some of the residents of Hollyville – the households with children – awoke to find boxes of John's toys had been left on their doorstep. The racing car was left to little Jim Gerarty who lived at the other number eight. Knowing its provenance, the Gerarty boy treasured that car throughout his childhood years.

Occasionally the MacElhinney brothers would be given a lift to school with the Bale family at number seven. Formality would be followed when knocking at the door and, on top of that, when it was answered they would be expected to speak the *cúpla focail* of Irish, the language of the house. Lorcan Bale hardly ever spoke, a silence that the visitors found quite intimidating. The other Bale siblings, by contrast, were quite outgoing: just very normal children who were happy to chat about whatever happened to be on their minds on any given day.

Some neighbours found it amusing – and a little bit odd – that the Bale children would be summoned home at mealtimes by the blowing of a whistle. They certainly were very different from many of their neighbours: the fact that they were an Irish-speaking family would have immediately set them apart. Most Irish people have a reasonable understanding of Irish, but at that time there were relatively few households outside of the native Irish-speaking *Gaeltacht* areas where Irish would have been the first language of the home. Kenneth Bale was an academic, who held not only a masters degree in Irish but was also conversant in Latin. For 16 years he worked as a teacher at Mount Melleray Abbey School, an establishment run by Cistercian monks in County Waterford on Ireland's south coast. For someone who was so painfully shy, standing up in front of a class to teach Irish must have been very difficult for the young Mr Bale. A devout Catholic and an enthusiastic supporter of the Church on moral matters, he would have been born a Protestant had not his father, while working for the Royal Mail in pre-independence Ireland, converted to Catholicism. Indeed many of Kenneth Bale's church friends would have been surprised had they ever learned that one of his ancestors was an Anglican bishop.

Mr Bale was always neatly dressed. He wore a freshly pressed shirt each day, with a tie fashioned into a tiny knot, and he occasionally finished off the look by donning a Sherlock Holmes-style deerstalker hat. While Sir Arthur Conan Doyle's fictional detective accessorised with a curved pipe, Mr Bale smoked Caltas – fiercely strong unfiltered Spanish cigarettes, a long obsolete brand with an overbearing pungency. He did, quite sensibly, eventually quit. His choice of cigarette may not have been driven by flavour alone: Mr Bale was an Hispanophile, a lover of all things Spanish. He taught himself Spanish by listening to the radio, yet there are no records of this skilled linguist ever having left Ireland, so it is doubtful that he ever set foot in his beloved Spain. He spoke enthusiastically about Spain's dictator, General Franco, a violently repressive head of state who ruled with an iron fist from 1936 to his death in 1975. Mr Bale's reverence towards Franco could have been due to the dictator upholding the Catholic Church as the established church of the Spanish state. This recognition restored several long lost privileges to Catholics in Spain. Civil servants had to be Catholic, indeed certain official positions even required a 'good behaviour letter' signed by a priest. Civil marriages that had taken place in republican Spain were declared null and void unless confirmed by the Catholic Church, a difficult if not impossible requirement considering civil marriages had only been provided after the couple had made a public renunciation of the Catholic faith. Divorce was forbidden, as were the sale of contraceptives and the practice of abortion. In his later years Mr Bale would become a highly vocal opponent of what he saw as the creeping liberalism invading Ireland; his later writings reveal that he believed liberalism to be an insidious doctrine, one he imagined was led by homosexuals and included promiscuous users of contraceptives, fornicators, abortionists and opponents of the sanctity of Catholic matrimony.

After leaving his teaching job in circumstances unknown – one account refers to him as a 'resigned teacher' – Mr Kenneth Bale gained a coveted secure job in the Irish civil service. This was in every sense a job for life: decent pay, increments each year, virtually unsackable and with a generous final salary pension scheme guaranteed on retirement. The division to which Mr Bale was attached was the Ordnance Survey (the OS), responsible for creating official maps of Ireland. His job was a specialist one: as a Higher Placenames Officer, he was part of a small team responsible for correctly naming townlands, villages and hamlets in the Irish language across the Republic of Ireland's 26 counties. It was a job perfectly suited to his skills. The work was slow and required a great deal of academic research, often drawing from the archives of John O'Donovan, a nineteenth-century Irish scholar whose detailed studies of place names helped to standardise the titles and spellings of the country's townlands. The OS was housed in Mountjoy House, an imposing stone manse built in 1724, restored in the nineteenth century and now semi-derelict. It stands in Dublin's Phoenix Park, one of the largest walled urban parks in Europe, whose few residents include *Uachtarán na hÉireann* – The President of Ireland – and also the Ambassador of the United States to Ireland. The OS was quite unlike other civil service departments: most men joined from the army where they had gained specialist mapping knowledge in the army surveyor corps. In those days, the word 'nepotism' was not in the vernacular. People spoke about the OS being a family tradition. Staff were proud of the fact that their fathers and grandfathers right back to the days of British rule were steeped in OS heritage. Occasionally, in this working community, effectively isolated from the outside world by its location in Phoenix Park, relationships would develop, which would in some cases lead to marriage, children and a potential new generation of OS staff. Women rarely rose much above secretarial level – indeed if a secretary were to get married, she would be compelled to resign her job as part of a system known as the 'marriage bar', a practice only outlawed in 1977. It really was a man's world. In the early '70s four young women were recruited to the OS from outside of the civil service system to work as specialist cartographers. Their male colleagues, seeing these young women in their late teens being asked to do what they considered to be a man's job, refused point blank to work with them. A standoff followed where the men continued to work and the four women spent their days chatting, reading and drinking tea in the staff canteen. After six months of stalemate, the women were quietly redeployed to other areas of the civil service and the status quo was restored.

Regardless of the importance of the work carried out in the Ordnance Survey Irish Placenames Section, it does not sound like a barrel of laughs. Some but not all of the staff were socially inept loners. One man shared an office with a colleague for months with hardly a word being exchanged between them. In Mr Bale's case, there was no friendly banter with colleagues. He was shy: on a good day he might acknowledge the presence of his colleagues, but most of the time he would keep his head down and do his job. He did occasionally spring to life when listening to the radio that sat on a mantelpiece in the office; colleagues recall him becoming quite animated when a right-wing campaigner on moral issues, Mena Bean uí Chribín, would make one of her regular appearances on the *Gay Byrne Hour*. Mr Bale and Bean uí Chribín shared broadly similar views on issues of morality, especially those concerned with family values. In her colourful life, the campaigner has denounced the Pope for being too liberal, condemned divorcees as adulterers, stated that contraception was a topic that simply should not be discussed and voiced equally forthright views on corporal punishment in schools, a widespread practice in the '70s and '80s. 'If a four- or five-year-old child decides to be bold, there's no power in heaven that'll stop that child from running around except a quick slap,' declared Mena Bean uí Chribín in a nationally broadcast interview. 'So to scrap that means that our lives are now governed by bold five- and six-year-old children. That's really what *they* have done.' But aside from these brief flashes of passion whenever a controversial moral point was debated on the radio, Mr Bale kept his own counsel and in his own quiet way did the job he was paid to do.

On Friday 15 June 1973, the Chief Placenames Officer called all of the staff together for an unscheduled meeting a few minutes after 10 a.m. There was one absentee, the Higher Placenames Officer Mr Kenneth Bale. 'I have to tell you something, as you will surely hear about it in any event,' declared the senior manager. 'It pains me to inform you that it appears that Ken's eldest son may have been involved in the death of a seven-year-old boy.' He directed them to a small article in the morning paper, above which was a black-and-white photo of a smiling John Horgan. 'Boy (7) is found dead,' was the headline. The story did little to convey the true ghastliness of the previous day's events. It would be a month before a broken Mr Bale would return to work to face his colleagues.

Back in Hollyville that same morning the two MacElhinney brothers awoke to see an unusual amount of police activity in the street. Eoin MacElhinney, who, like John Horgan, was aged seven at the time, remembers clearly being in his dressing gown and slippers looking out the kitchen window with his mother. There in the back field was Lorcan Bale, dressed in the same clothes he had worn the previous evening, walking slowly with two uniformed officers. Eoin was too young to fully comprehend what was happening, but the killer was retracing his steps, leading investigators to the murder spot, a large, overgrown hedge with hanging trees known by the Hollyville children as 'the hideout'. After breakfast, the MacElhinney brothers went to the Bale house, as they would normally have expected a lift to school from Mr Bale. The doorbell of number seven was answered by a burly man in uniform who politely told the boys that the Bales would not be going to school that day.

The following day, Saturday 16 June, was warm, cloudless and for most of the city's residents, the perfect start to the weekend. But in number six Hollyville, the atmosphere was altogether different. Most of the adults of this small community gathered in the Horgan house for the funeral Mass for the little boy. Mr Bale, visibly shaken, stood on one side of the room, the Horgans on the other. As the Mass reached its conclusion, the priest invited the group to give each other the Sign of Peace, when traditionally a handshake is accompanied by the words 'peace be with you'. At this point in the proceedings Mr Horgan crossed the room and faced Mr Bale. The taller man paused before raising both arms and embracing Mr Bale firmly. In response, Mr Bale wept uncontrollably. There was not a soul in the house that morning who was not visibly moved by the selfless generosity of this extraordinary gesture.

A month later Mr Bale returned to work without comment or ceremony. He would later move house to Home Farm Road in Glasnevin, a north Dublin suburb not far from the city centre. He never mentioned the murder to any of his workmates, who in turn never raised the subject. In that short period of four weeks, Mr Bale had visibly aged. He was carrying a burden no parent should ever have to carry and its weight was clearly taking its toll. As the murder trial of his eldest son approached, Mr Bale would sit quietly at his desk in the OS, positioned in a quiet corner of the Georgian building, the bay window surround lit by autumn sunshine. The atmosphere could best be described as tense: colleagues knew he was suffering, but somehow they could not find the right words to comfort him. Several times a day the Higher Placenames Officer would fall asleep, most likely a side effect of prescription medication given to provide relief to his shattered nerves. At around the same time, he stopped driving his car and commuted to Phoenix Park by bus. He never drove again.

After the trial Mr Bale retreated further into his own private world. A new office routine was added to his practice of solitary working and sleeping on the job. That was prayer. A more junior colleague recalled that many of Mr Bale's waking hours were spent quietly reciting alternative Hail Marys and Our Fathers, a well-thumbed set of rosary beads clutched in his wiry hands. While physically present, he became ever more reclusive, far from being a team player in the division. Within the organisation there was a strict pecking order, a seniority structure understood and respected by all staff. So when the Chief Placenames Officer died suddenly, Mr Bale, as a Higher Placenames Officer and the number two in the department, would under normal circumstances have been the natural successor. This matter was not addressed until after the funeral, when Kenneth Bale without fuss let it be quietly known that he would not be a candidate for the position. Colleagues believed that Mr Bale recognised that the social interaction, which was an essential element of the role, was now just too much for him. The murder had clearly altered him physically and emotionally. Despite being in his mid 50s, the memories of one former workmate were of a man who looked as though he should have been long retired. At work he demonstrated all the characteristics of a broken man, though outside of the OS, members of the prayer group that he attended described him as a storyteller with a great sense of humour, indeed they emphasised his outgoing personality.

Talking to Mr Bale's contemporaries, one comes across a picture of the Ordnance Survey of Ireland as a rich and rewarding place to work in the '70s: an imposing Georgian mansion in a huge scenic park, where fallow deer would roam freely in the grounds, an environment that was at times eccentric, made more so by the gifted people that contributed to its success. Despite the sedentary nature of the work, there were occasional moments of drama, including one notable incident involving Mr Bale.

The OS was not a place for early starters. It was usually 10 a.m. before the full complement of staff were at their desks. Lunch was taken for an hour around 1 p.m., while the day wound to a close at 4.45 p.m. A couple of years after the trial, on a date long forgotten, Mr Bale was first to arrive in the office, at what must have been shortly after 9 a m. Next to show was a bright young academic researcher, Cathal Goan, who, like Kenneth Bale, was a fluent Irish speaker. Goan's wife, Maighread Ní Dhomhnaill, a highly regarded traditional Irish singer, was at the time a theatre nurse at Dublin's Mount Carmel Hospital, the very same suburban hospital where John Horgan was born a few years earlier. From routinely chatting to his wife about her day-to-day work at Mount Carmel, Cathal Goan had – more by stealth than design – picked up the rudiments of first aid, skills that were to prove life saving in this instance. On that particular morning in the OS, young Cathal Goan ambled into the library to find Mr Bale semi-conscious, face down on the floor. Recognising immediately that the older man was displaying all the classic symptoms of a heart attack, Goan placed him in the recovery position, loosened his clothing and propped up his head with a bulky encyclopedia pulled from the library shelves. He had to wait a few minutes for the telephone switchboard operator to clock in before he could dial 999. The ambulance duly arrived outside and rushed Mr Bale to hospital where after intensive treatment he recovered. He owed his life to the prompt actions of Cathal Goan. The young researcher went on to have a glittering career in television, eventually, in 2003, reaching the top position in Irish broadcasting, director-general of the state broadcaster, Raidió Teilifís Éireann.

Kenneth Bale's near-death experience served if anything to harden his opinions about the erosion of the nation's morals and the creeping secularism that he viewed as a slow-moving pandemic infecting the country. Through the '70s there was vigorous public debate in Ireland about many of life's most passionate issues, matters that had until that time been regarded as settled or beyond dispute, including questions of sex, sexuality and the Church, and questions of gender, morality and change. Families were split on many issues and morality was the chief topic of discussion in many of the nation's homes, churches and pubs. The questions that were being asked challenged the very structure of the state. Questions including: should contraception be made available, and if so, to whom? To bona fide married couples or freely to anyone who wants to control their fertility? Divorce was another thorny issue. Outlawed by the Irish constitution, any change in the law would need not just parliamentary approval but also a referendum, a nationwide poll of the people. There were other equally controversial issues: homosexual acts were illegal in Ireland under laws dating back to Victorian times. Abortion was also illegal, the blanket ban being enforced under the Offences against the Person Act 1861. Kenneth Bale took a deeply conservative view on all of these issues. We know this to be the case because he was a vigorous letter writer to Irish newspapers; a trawl through the dusty microfiches in Dublin's National Library reveals no fewer than 21 letters to the editor penned by Mr Bale in both Irish and English. While today his views might appear to be somewhat extreme, for their time they were quite mainstream, so would be better read as a snapshot of conservative thinking of the day rather than the ramblings of a crank.

> A chara,
> I find it incredible that a Dáil whose members are predominantly Catholic should even give consideration to a bill that enables young people (whether they begin at 16 or 18) to commit fornication and avoid the consequences through committing an additional sin of preventing conception by unnatural means. It is time for Catholic voters and all who value Christian moral standards to make their voices heard.
> Mise le meas
> Kenneth Bale

This letter was in opposition to the Health (Family Planning) Bill that was introduced by the then Taoiseach (prime minister) Charles Haughey. This bill limited the provision of contraceptives purely for 'family planning or for adequate medical reasons'. Controversially the law proposed that contraceptives could only be dispensed by a pharmacist on the presentation of a valid doctor's prescription. While some believe this was a restriction that penalised the very people who most needed easy access to contraception, for others, like Mr Bale, it was a bill too far. The law did not require the 'patient' to be married, but in practice unmarried couples and singles wanting to get hold of a pack of condoms found the humiliation of the entire experience to be a significant deterrent. The Roman Catholic Church, which was deeply influential in the country, lobbied heavily for the maintenance of the status quo, and this effectively prohibited the government from producing a more liberal law. In a phrase that has long stood the test of time, Haughey famously described the Act as 'an Irish solution to an Irish problem'.

The use of condoms once again came to the fore with the sudden appearance of the HIV virus and resultant AIDS-related deaths. With infection rates increasing rapidly, most particularly among gay men and intravenous drug users, it was clear that something had to be done, and done quickly. The gravity of the condition was brought home to many by the passing of one of Ireland's best loved television presenters, Vincent 'Fab Vinnie' Hanley, who was the first Irish celebrity to die from an AIDS-related illness – though this was not fully acknowledged until years later, such was the stigma. The government was under pressure to put moral objections to condoms to one side, given the breadth of evidence stating that the safe use of condoms could dramatically cut the risk of infection. Kenneth Bale – and others – begged to differ.

> A chara,
> Your recent editorial on AIDS (3 March) adopts the attitude that in dealing with a matter of national urgency, the moral law may be set aside as being irrelevant. Thank God, the great mass of the Irish people continue loyal to the Judeo-Christian standards of morality enshrined in our constitution. The results of two referendums bear witness to this fact.
> Mise le meas
> Kenneth Bale

The two referendums referred to were a successful attempt to have a ban on abortion copper-fastened to the Irish constitution, and an attempt to introduce divorce to Ireland.

> A chara,
> This is not the only sphere in which the secularists would like the freedom of the individual and the family. We have seen their efforts to deprive parents of the right to have a say on who teaches their children and what kind of moral formation they are given at school. If a

referendum on divorce is to take place, let the people of
Ireland understand what is involved. A vote for divorce
is a step in a direction of state totalitarianism.
Mise le meas
Kenneth Bale

The divorce referendum campaign was a bitter battle, a verbal
slog fought on the airwaves and in the newspapers. Being largely
an agricultural nation, there were fears that the possible
introduction of divorce would result in the breaking up of the
Irish family farm, traditionally passed down the generations
through the eldest son. The referendum was resoundingly
defeated, and Kenneth Bale would not live long enough to see
the ban eventually removed by the slimmest of margins: 50.2 per
cent in favour of a new divorce law to 49.7 per cent against.

But the bitterest of arguments was reserved for the various
abortion referendum campaigns. Abortion remains illegal in Ireland
and it appears, for the moment at least, that the majority of Irish
people reject the notion of abortion on demand. But in the '70s
and '80s, conservative campaigners – including Kenneth Bale –
feared that having lost the battle on contraception, as well as being
able to foresee the relaxing of bans on homosexual relations and on
seeking a divorce, the next logical step could be the introduction of
abortion to Ireland. For Mr Bale, this was a step too far.

A chara,
The fact that a wave of immorality is passing over our
country should not be taken as an excuse for jettisoning
these standards but should rather be seen as emphasising
the need of reasserting them. The ordinary people of the
Republic have declared their loyalty in two referendums
in which they frustrated the attempts of small pressure
groups to impose their views on the majority.
Mise le meas
Kenneth Bale

Most of the Bale letters, however, are on the subject of the Irish language. Mr Bale was passionate about the language, its rich history and its place in the nation's cultural wealth. In the letter columns, he swiped at anyone who felt that Irish was in any way a lesser language than other European languages, including English. He also was critical of teachers who in his view were not sufficiently versed in the tongue. Yet another of his concerns was exposing children to teachers who did not share his own particular religious views.

> A chara
> I should like to point out that it is a fundamental right of parents of any religion to have their children educated according to the doctrines and principles of that religion. It would be an act of the gravest injustice towards Christian parents to force them to have their children taught by atheists or by people who are leading immoral lives.
> Mise le meas
> Kenneth Bale

At no point in the letters does the reader get even the slightest hint of the personal turmoil that the writer must surely have been experiencing. He never once wrote about the dangers of the occult, which, given the fact that his eldest son was a self-professed satanist who had killed an innocent child as part of an obscene ritual, seems to be a surprising omission. There was also no suggestion that perhaps Mr Bale himself may have had any failings as a parent, instead he reserved his vitriol for others who did not live up to his own perceived exacting standards.

On an autumn day in 1989, Kenneth Bale suffered a second, more acute heart attack which this time claimed his life. He was aged just 67, yet those who knew him would say he looked much older. After the funeral Mass, his remains were laid to rest in Glasnevin cemetery, sharing a common resting place with some of

Ireland's most prominent national figures including playwright Brendan Behan as well as political leaders including Charles Stewart Parnell, Michael Collins and a man with whom Mr Bale would surely have shared many views, former Irish President Éamon de Valera. His modest square granite headstone stands above an unfussy patch of ground dusted with dead leaves and a few hardy weeds. Tucked in a corner at the eastern end of the cemetery, the gravestone is inscribed in old Irish.

> I Bhuan Cuimhne Kenneth Bale. 26th May 1922 – 13th Oct 1989. Mairfidh ár ngrath go h-éag na bhláth síor ur. Reqisescat in Pacé.

Translated it reads:

> In Eternal Memory of Kenneth Bale. 26th May 1922 – 13th Oct 1989. Our love will survive until the forever fresh flowers die. Rest in Peace.

His last will and testament, written shortly after his retirement from the OS, is in Irish. Writing an important legal document in Irish is not at all uncommon for someone with the expertise in and passion for the language that Kenneth Bale held. Translated it reads:

> I, Kenneth Gordon Bale, 131 Home Farm Road, Dublin, declare this is my last will and testament. With this will I revoke any wills I have made previously. I appoint my wife Catherine as executor of this will, and direct her to clear any debts I may have outstanding and to pay from my estate my funeral costs.
>
> I bequeath all my wealth to my wife Catherine to be used for her own welfare.
>
> Signed in the presence of witnesses. Kenneth G Bale. 26th October 1982.

# THREE

## Thick as Thieves

Lorcan Bale's childhood was punctuated by significant illnesses, and this had a profound effect on his schooling. Most Irish children begin secondary school at around age 11. But it was September 1971, when he was aged 14, before Lorcan entered Coláiste Mhuire, a prestigious fee-paying school in Dublin city centre. Coláiste Mhuire was quite different to most schools in the locality: firstly, as it was outside the free education sector, it attracted a generally middle-class intake. Secondly, all subjects, with the exception of English, were taught through Irish. Language and religion were at the very core of the school's ethos: history, geography and science lessons took place entirely in Irish, and exams were conducted in the language, a strategy actively encouraged by the government of the day, whose education department awarded extra credit for pupils who took their examinations in Irish. It went further: speaking English was not just frowned upon, it was a punishable offence, with rule breakers facing the discipline of the leather strap. Britain and all things English were deemed to be pernicious influences. One contemporary, Brendan Thomas, recalled that on weekly Wednesday sports days, kicking but not picking up the ball would single out a boy for punishment – this was a giveaway sign that the boy was playing soccer, a wicked English game, as opposed to Ireland's beloved national sport, Gaelic football, in which the ball is both kicked and held.

Established by Roman Catholic Christian Brothers in 1931 with the purpose of providing secondary level education through Irish, Coláiste Mhuire had – and still has – a tradition of high academic achievement. The alumnae include an impressive list of well-known figures in business, politics, academia, music, sport and the broadcast media. In the '70s, this all-boys school was sited in Parnell Square next to the Hugh Lane Gallery of Modern Art. The year 1995 saw a transforming change of policy, the beginning of the admission of girls, and by 2005 the Parnell Square site was abandoned in favour of a gleaming modern campus in Cabra, some three miles to the north.

When I approached Coláiste Mhuire for information about Lorcan Bale's schooldays, the request was politely declined. The principal, speaking through a secretary, said that, 'Lorcan Bale had a very sad life, one that was tragic', adding, 'all this was a long time ago, and I don't want to hear any more'. However several of the boy's classmates have shown no such reluctance and were more than happy to share their memories – it is from their testimonies we can piece together the events of Lorcan Bale's unconventional schooldays. Indeed, it is highly illuminating when recounting the story of Lorcan Bale to consider the mindset of his best friend at school – indeed his only friend – a boy who shared the same Christian name: Lorcan Conroy.

In the course of my research I had heard the name – Conroy was one of a number of people of Lorcan Bale's age who had known the teenage killer. Many former classmates of Bale's mentioned Conroy as a person who knew Lorcan Bale well and could perhaps shed some light on his character and state of mind. It was essential that I tracked him down, but where to start? As a child, he had lived in Lucan, just a few miles west of Palmerstown. Door-to-door enquiries drew a blank. A few days later I came across an email address for a Lorcan Conroy, who may or may not have been the right Lorcan Conroy. Nonetheless, it was well worth a punt.

From: David Malone
To: Lorcan Conroy
Subject: Long Shot
Dear Lorcan,
I came across your email address this week. – Not sure if you're the person I'm looking for. It's a long shot.

I work as a TV producer and writer, making factual programmes for a range of broadcasters including the BBC, RTÉ and Channel 4.

At the moment I am researching a book which includes events surrounding a murder that took place in Palmerstown in 1973.

If you're the Lorcan Conroy who lived at Lucan Heights, you may be able to help with my research. If not, I do apologise for bothering you.

If however this is you, would you mind getting in touch – in confidence. My contacts are below.

With best regards,
David

Less than 24 hours later, my inbox pinged, signifying the arrival of a new message.

From: Lorcan Conroy
To: David Malone
Subject: Re – Long Shot
Hi David,
Sometimes long shots pay off. I am indeed the person you are looking for. I would be happy to talk to you about the incident you refer to. Let's have a chat first and we'll take it from there.

I look forward to hearing from you.
Regards,
Lorcan Conroy

At the foot of the mail was his number and address. He had moved from Lucan, but only to a town about an hour's drive away. We agreed to meet in a hotel the next afternoon.

The bar was dark, with workmen carrying out badly needed renovations. At 3 p.m. precisely a thin man in his early 50s, with longish hair and a cheeky smile bounded over to the table where I was sitting. 'You must be David,' he stated, offering his hand. Over the next couple of hours we spent time getting to know each other, and teasing out the relationship between Lorcan Conroy and his namesake, Lorcan Bale. Over the following weeks we had a number of further interview sessions, both face to face and on the phone. Conroy's memories of a misspent youth were filled with colourful details, a snapshot not just of events, but of the era: Dublin in the '70s. The accuracy of his recall was primarily due to the fact that some years ago he considered writing a book about his schooldays and had already committed a great deal to paper. His is a perspective on the murder of the Horgan boy that nobody else could offer, and perhaps in due course a publisher will encourage him to finish the work. We got on well and after the whole story had been told, in at times frantic detail, I asked him to tell it all again, this time from the beginning.

Three months younger than Bale, Lorcan Conroy was born in the Coombe Hospital, situated in what was at the time a rundown district of inner-city Dublin. The eldest of four children, his early years in the suburb of Drimnagh were uneventful, and when he was seven the family moved to Lucan, a pretty village on the outskirts of the city. The family had clearly moved up in the world: Mr Conroy had a good job as a door-to-door insurance salesman with the brokerage Irish Life, and business was steady. Like any parent, Lorcan Conroy's father wanted the best for his children, and he decided at the outset that they were not to be educated at the free local school in the company of ruffians. Rather the Conroy clan would have what Mr Conroy had never received: a private education. So it was that aged just seven, Lorcan Conroy was enrolled at Coláiste Mhuire.

From the first day, the Conroy boy hated the school. All of his friends had gone to the local, free, national primary school and, through Lorcan's eyes, had an education where they seemed to enjoy every moment. He did not make friends in Coláiste Mhuire; being a wheezy asthmatic meant he was poor at sport, which excluded him from any hope of popularity and made him an easy target for bullies. Neither was he academic – he had a low attention span and little interest in his studies. A knack for attracting trouble did not endear him to his teachers, and this was a time when the casual brutalities of the cane and the strap were still widespread. School seemed to Lorcan Conroy like a long, tedious punishment, one that he had done nothing to deserve.

The summer of 1971 was unusually warm, and its end was met with dread by Lorcan Conroy as he took the dreary morning bus journey to Dublin, ready for the first day of the new term. As the miles ticked by he daydreamed he would arrive to discover that the school had been levelled in one of the bomb attacks that had left their recent mark on the city due to the Northern Ireland conflict. But it was a short walk from the bus stop to the four-story Victorian block at Parnell Square, and his hopes were soon dashed, for the school loomed up before him, depressingly whole. Stubbing out his last cigarette and resigning himself to another year of misery, Lorcan made his way to a second-floor classroom. From their third year, all pupils were streamed: the brighter ones were allocated to the 'A stream', while those who were less academic found themselves in the 'L stream'. Lorcan Conroy, to no one's surprise, including his own, had been placed in the L stream. It was never made clear what the 'L' stood for – 'lower', perhaps – but to students at Coláiste Mhuire, in whatever class, the 'L' was understood to mean 'losers'. Conroy preferred to think of it as the 'life' class, for those who were too busy experiencing real life to bother with the tedious humdrum of academia.

Walking into the classroom, he found that on each double desk were two names, indicating the place where each pupil would spend the next three terms. His name was positioned in the middle of the second row, uncomfortably close to the front of the class, to his mind. They always found some way to make school worse for you. Sitting down, he leaned to his right to read the name on the desk next to his own. To his surprise, it was a name he did not recognise, a pupil new to Coláiste Mhuire, Lorcan Bale. They even shared the same Christian name.

Their teacher strode into the room to the sounds of scraping chairs and squeaking shoes as 20 or so boys stood up. Known to all as 'Jagger', his subject was mathematics, and he was one of very few lay teachers working at the school. Unlike his Christian Brother colleagues he had a reputation for being sparing with the leather strap. Jagger was also by far the coolest teacher in the school, a throwback from the '60s who sported a suede cowboy jacket, shoulder-length hair and flared trousers. But he was no pushover. The lesson began with a stern lecture on the importance of punctuality, including a 'three strikes and you're out' warning to latecomers. The nature of the punishment was not specified but every boy present was left in no doubt that it would be very unpleasant. This done, the lesson – and the year – commenced.

Ten minutes into the lesson the door swung open and a gaunt, lanky figure strolled into the classroom. With a cursory nod of apology to the teacher, Lorcan Bale made his way to the desk that he and Lorcan Conroy would be sharing. He could not have known how particularly untimely his late entrance was. Conroy surveyed the new boy's demeanour: five foot six inches tall, he was startlingly thin, with pale, sunken eyes and long fair hair that looked as though it had never seen a comb. To try and give some bulk to his cadaverous form he wore a black leather biker's jacket, purple flares and beige Hush Puppies – none of which was at all 'cool', and all of which immediately marked him as different from his classmates.

The two boys used their lunch break to get to know each other. Speaking English in defiance of the strict 'Irish only' school rule, it was clear they had much in common. Conroy lived in Lucan;

Bale in the next village, Palmerstown, meaning they would share the bus journeys in the morning and afternoon. Both boys were asthmatic, with Bale's condition the more severe, requiring him to carry an inhaler. Despite this they also both smoked, indeed they had the same choice of brand: the high tar Churchmans Number 1, marketed as 'the 15-minute cigarette'. They even liked the same music: David Bowie, Slade, also metal rockers Alice Cooper and Black Sabbath. By the time the bell went for the return to class, each Lorcan had found a soul mate.

Maybe this year wouldn't be so bad after all?

The first year that the two lads spent together was peppered with several misdemeanours that would be common to many a youngster disillusioned with school and seeking a little excitement in their lives. Neither student was particularly academic, and both would occasionally play truant from school. These days would be spent hanging around Dublin city centre, their favourite haunts being the leafy lawns of St Stephen's Green, and the city's most upmarket shopping avenue, Grafton Street. Lorcan Bale was a regular at a small oriental store, next to the Dandelion Market, where a few short years later a young up-and-coming teenage band called U2 would entertain a handful of supporters happy to pay the entrance fee of just 30 pence. In the Indian Bazaar, Bale would buy joss sticks, candles, and books on meditation. At this stage these were innocent purchases, though they marked Bale out as seeking to differentiate himself from the mainstream.

When they did attend school, the two Lorcans paid scant regard to the rules. Pupils today would be shocked at what was considered acceptable in the '70s, and what was not: while playing soccer was banned, smoking was permitted for senior pupils. Bale and Conroy were still in the intermediate school and prohibited from smoking, but they didn't let this stop them. As well as bending the rules, the boys tried to liven up their school lives with pranks. Classmates recall a Latin class held by a teacher known as 'Helen of Troy'. Lorcan Bale decided that, for kicks, he would spend the entire class hidden in the wardrobe at the corner of the classroom.

All the other pupils were aware of his presence, having helped him seal himself inside just moments before the teacher's arrival at the beginning of class. Half an hour into the lesson, the class was disturbed by a sudden thud from inside the wardrobe. The teacher opened the door and Lorcan Bale spilled out, collapsing on the cold wooden floor, to the wild hilarity of the other students. Half an hour of breathing inside the small, stuffy space had caused the asthmatic teenager to pass out from lack of oxygen. Luckily, after only a few gasps of his inhaler and a little fresh air, Bale was soon recovering and could be sent for punishment.

By autumn 1972 the boys had been thick as thieves for a year and were becoming ever more daring in their quest for new adventures. Both were desperate to lose their virginities, but their many attempts were met with failure: neither could even talk properly to a girl, never mind charm one into a lustful tryst. It was hard for two awkward teenagers attending an all-boys school to meet girls. The most desirable girls were those attending King's Hospital, an upmarket, largely Protestant school where the girls – unusually for the time – wore shockingly revealing 'short' skirts – ones that showed their actual legs. According to male adolescent rumour, these girls were more willing than most to Do It, but for some reason none of the girls Conroy or Bale spoke to seemed to share this understanding.

King's Hospital – close to the Bale home in Palmerstown – was also the scene for an early criminal enterprise. Perpetually short of the money they needed to buy cigarettes, magazines and cinema tickets, the two Lorcans cooked up an elaborate plan to steal a racing cycle and sell it to a willing buyer from their school. Bale set about finding an appropriate bike, and on one of his forays to King's Hospital he noticed that a shiny new racer was locked at the same time each evening to railings outside the school's swimming pool. A plan was hatched, and days later the boys found themselves walking in the dark through the grounds of the boarding school. Bale had a silver hacksaw, and while his accomplice Conroy kept watch for passers by, he quickly sawed through the lock while the bike's unfortunate owner was having his evening swim. Within minutes the bike was in Lorcan Bale's garage, where it remained for several weeks until the buyer arrived to collect his stolen goods. Promising to pay 40 pounds for the high performance racer, this buyer took it away and painted it matt pink. But he never paid the young thieves, much to their annoyance. Lorcan Conroy recalled,

> The bike was really beautiful, but when that guy painted it pink it just looked like a stolen bike. To make matters worse, a couple of weeks later the theft was featured on *Garda Patrol*, a police appeal TV series that seemed to feast on petty crimes – stolen tractors and the like. My heart sank when that came on the telly. I felt like a wanted man.

Bale's next theft was to prove much more risky. It was December 1972 and Ireland was suffering a particularly harsh winter. One morning during the school lunch break, the two Lorcans were huddled together in the playground sneaking a cigarette. Lorcan Conroy was feeling the cold most – he had just lost his third pair of gloves, and his mother refused to buy him any more. School, he felt, was miserable at the best of times, but doubly miserable right then. He looked over to see Bale staring intently at a window in the main school building, and Conroy could see from his eyes that his namesake was scheming. Later, on the bus home, Bale revealed his plan – the boys would have cash for Christmas. All he needed to do was to break into the school secretary's office and steal the cash box containing money collected for school outings and other extracurricular expenses. Whatever Conroy felt about the appeal of having a full wallet, he decided at that point that this was a crime too far.

'You're out of your tiny fucking mind!' he blurted. Bale's smirk faded as his eyes froze to an icy stare.

'So you think I have a tiny mind do you? You stupid prick. Don't you ever laugh at me again you fucking moron or I'll tear your fucking head off. I'll show you who's got the tiny mind around here. You just watch me.' With that, he turned away. Conroy had seen enough flashes of Bale's temper before to know he had to back off. He said nothing more.

Next morning Conroy barely spoke to his deskmate during class. This continued until lunchtime that Friday when the pair headed to the Borza Café, a greasy spoon Italian diner popular with the Coláiste Mhuire crowd. Bale bought two large plates of thick-cut chips and placed them on one of the red plastic tables.

'Well?' asked Conroy. Bale ignored him and reached for the ketchup. Then, having teased him enough, the older boy smiled and relented.

'OK, I'll tell you,' he said.

And so over their lunch of chips and cola, Lorcan Bale recounted the events of the previous evening, events that began shortly after his parents had gone to bed. The teenager had assembled a small rucksack with the tools that his mission demanded: a sleeping bag, a roll of duct tape and a small rock hammer – the type that a geologist might use to collect fossil samples. Next he spent some time making sure that his bike was running well, paying particular attention to the dynamo that powered the lights. After all he did not want to be stopped by the police for such a trivial matter as faulty lights, not when he had bigger crimes in mind. Dressed entirely in black, he pedalled silently into the night, away from Palmerstown on the six-mile journey to Dublin. The evening was clear and with no traffic to speak of the trip took a little over half an hour. Near the school at O'Connell Street, the city's main thoroughfare, he passed a police patrol car on its way to a disturbance outside a pub that had closed its doors minutes earlier. Bale pedalled on until he reached a tiny lane at the back of the school; there were no streetlights here, and the silence and darkness made it eerie. Earlier that day, he had positioned an oil barrel that was discarded in the lane against the school wall. The placement was careful and deliberate. The top of the wall had shards of glass embedded in cement to prevent anyone from scaling it, but one small section below the barrel appeared to have very little glass. Bale climbed onto the barrel and folded his sleeping bag on the top of the wall. Placing the rucksack on his back, he hauled himself up, being careful not to cut his hands, and vaulted over the wall. The young aspiring burglar misjudged the distance and landed heavily on the concrete, severely winding himself. But living with asthma had taught Bale to control his breathing and after a couple of minutes he had regained his strength and composure. Walking across the silent playground, normally packed with students, he reached the office door. From his backpack, he removed the duct tape and rock hammer, first duct taping the window next to the door to avoid the potentially noisy shattering of glass. Then with a single knock of the hammer, the window gave way, allowing him to reach in and slip the lock. Moments later he was in the office. The cash box was in its usual place and, much to his delight, was unlocked. Bale ignored the cheques and general paperwork, but took every banknote and coin that he could see in the half light. Mission accomplished, he picked up a ladder from outside the caretaker's shed and used it to scale the wall where his bike was parked. Within an hour he was sitting on his bed at home, counting the results of his night's work.

'I can't remember exactly how much he got,' recalled Lorcan Conroy in the pub decades later, 'but to us it was a fortune.' Sipping his pint, he added, 'I think it was close to 100 pounds in notes and I couldn't believe that he even went to the trouble of taking all the change as well.'

If acquiring this small fortune required risk and effort, spending it would be far easier. The first opportunity to put a dent in the ill-gotten stash came days later as the two boys browsed the entertainment listings in the *Evening Press*. Their initial intention was to find a movie, preferably a French film that might allow them a glimpse of bare flesh, but immediately their eyes were drawn to the banner advertisement at the bottom of the page: 'LIVE IN CONCERT: SLADE PLUS SUPPORT. THE

NATIONAL STADIUM, DUBLIN.' Neither boy had ever been to a gig before, and the opportunity was one they could not miss. Bale announced that he would buy the tickets; the only potential problem was persuading their parents that they should be allowed to attend. Bale didn't end up having any difficulty in this regard. It is almost certain that Mr Bale would have point-blank refused such a request, so it is likely that his son offered an alternative explanation as to why he needed to go out that evening. Mr Conroy's reaction, however, was a tirade of abuse about performing English drug addicts corrupting Ireland's youth with a form of noise pollution that could never pass for music even in the darkest criminal low-life quarters. He categorically forbade his son to go. Lorcan Conroy had hoped his father would at least be open to the idea, and couldn't believe he had come so close, only to have the possibility torn away. He stormed off to his bedroom, miserable. Some minutes later, Mrs Conroy, seeing that her son had taken the refusal badly, knocked at the bedroom and asked her son to dry his tears before going downstairs to apologise to his father. This was too much for the boy who lashed out at his mother, accusing his parents of wrecking his life, adding that at the first available opportunity, he was moving out of home. Mrs Conroy went downstairs, and minutes later her husband entered the boy's bedroom to announce that he had reconsidered, the teenager could after all go to the concert, but that if he were to get arrested, he would be disowned by the family.

Though astonished by his victory, Lorcan Conroy casually told Lorcan Bale the next day that he had persuaded his parents to let him go to the gig. By this stage, tickets in hand, Bale was receiving offers of over twice face value for the sold out concert, but he declined all bids, even when the amounts became fanciful. For a brief period the two Lorcans had achieved a degree of popularity in the school, as other third years looked at them enviously. Conroy was pleased that in rejecting the lucrative ticket offers, Bale had stood by him. Indeed around this time Bale bought his friend an album, *Live in Europe*, by blues guitarist Rory Gallagher.

What Conroy did not appreciate at the time was that the equilibrium of their friendship had shifted, that these acts of generosity with stolen money had begun to give Bale the upper hand.

The fortnight dragged until eventually the boys found themselves at the National Stadium on Dublin's South Circular Road. More commonly used as a boxing ring, the stadium was occasionally used as a venue for visiting Irish show bands including Brendan Bowyer, Glen Curtin and the legendary Dickie Rock, nicknamed by his adoring fans as 'Spit on me Dickie'. But Slade were international rock and roll, glam rock megastars, and from the moment the curtain rose, the crowd were enraptured. Standing on their seats for a better view, the two teenagers from west Dublin sang their hearts out to hits including 'Mama Weer All Crazee Now' and the number one single 'Cum On Feel the Noize', a defining roar in the classic Slade mould. The venue was packed with skinheads clad in the uniform of blue denim jackets known as 'wides' and Doc Marten boots. It was also the first time that the boys had ever seen rock chicks, heavily made-up girls wearing tight shirts and tiny denim miniskirts that left very little to the boys' fertile young imaginations. The air was heavy with the musky sweat of thousands of revellers, tempered only by the unmistakable wafting scent of marijuana. In the minds of the two Lorcans, they had at last truly arrived, this was without doubt the greatest night of their young lives. Mr Conroy and Mr Bale, had they been there, would have hated every moment.

In his first year at Coláiste Mhuire, Lorcan Bale's grades were unremarkable, but acceptable nonetheless. By Christmas of 1972 his marks had slipped, and with the Intermediate Certificate just six months away, his parents became increasingly concerned. What they were not aware of was the degree to which their son was playing truant from the school, the fact that he held many of his teachers in contempt and that while he hoped desperately for academic success, he made little effort to translate this desire into hard work.

Wednesday was a prime truanting day for both Lorcans. At Coláiste Mhuire, rain or shine, Wednesday afternoon was devoted to either Gaelic football or hurling. Neither boy excelled at either game. Indeed because of their physical immaturity when compared to other boys in their year, they were simply incapable of coping with the rough and tumble of two of the world's most physical sports. To be fair to their teachers, they recognised this inherent weakness and allowed the two teenagers to opt out of ball games and spend the afternoon long distance running, pounding endless laps of the football pitch where the other boys played.

Winter had tightened its icy grip upon the city and this Wednesday was not a day that any boy would choose to run dozens of laps around a cold, bleak pitch. Lorcan Bale announced to his friend that he had deliberately left his sports gear at home as that very afternoon they were going to the cinema instead. Truanting was illegal, yet while it was not officially condoned in Coláiste Mhuire, there was a tacit acceptance by some teachers that a small number of pupils, notably those in the L class, would occasionally bunk off and there was little that could or should be done about it.

First stop that day was Connolly Rail Station where the boys secured their bags in a left luggage locker to avoid being easily identified as schoolboys. They could have gone to the Savoy, the Ambassador or Carlton Cinemas to see blockbusters such as *The Godfather* (1972), *Deliverance* (1972) or *Cabaret* (1972). But instead, they headed for the Green Cinema, which specialised in showing less popular art house films. It would be quite wrong to suggest that either boy had an appetite for the more obscure examples of film noir; rather they knew that at the Green they might see a film that revealed a touch of nudity, an almost unheard of vice in '70s Ireland.

The official film censor took his job very seriously, protecting the public from images that could offend their moral or religious sensibilities, so nudity of any form, except possibly in the most artistic sense, was consigned to the cutting-room floor. Around this time state broadcaster RTÉ carried a television drama called *The Spike*, charting the fictional workings of a tough Dublin inner-city school, far harsher than a place like Coláiste Mhuire. In the fifth episode viewers were treated to an evening art class where adults were learning the skills of life drawing. Carefully filmed to avoid showing the naked form of a young woman modelling for the students, the camera was cautiously positioned behind frosted glass, so that all the details of the model's nudity were blurred. However, she was naked, and viewers could see that she was naked. In that precise moment, when actress Madelyn Erskine cast aside her silk shawl, *The Spike* was doomed.

In the following days, all hell broke loose. The press rounded on RTÉ, whose switchboard was jammed with complaints from irate viewers. Motions of condemnation of the programme were passed by County Councils throughout the country. J.B. Murray, head of the right-wing pressure group the League of Decency, suffered a heart attack while phoning the papers to complain about the nude scene. Mr Murray's tearful wife told reporters that his family had tried to stop him from watching it, but he insisted on doing so. Under such extreme pressure, RTÉ dropped *The Spike* mid series. Even the then prime minister, Jack Lynch, joined in the outrage expressing his support for the decision to axe *The Spike*, despite never having seen it.

So it was against this moral backdrop that 15-year-old Lorcan Bale and his classmate Lorcan Conroy attempted to gain entry to the afternoon double bill: *The Grasshopper* (1969) and *Stigma* (1972). The film posters outside the Green Cinema looked enticing: *The Grasshopper*, starring Jacqueline Bisset and Jim Brown, promised a racy plot in which Christine Adams, a cheerful and innocent 19 year old from British Columbia, Canada, travels to Los Angeles to be with her fiancé, who works there in a bank. When the relationship doesn't work out, she moves to Las Vegas where before long she finds work as a showgirl. Then tragedy strikes and young Christine ends up a prostitute.

The other half of the double bill was *Stigma* – a low-budget movie starring Philip Michael Thomas, later to find fame as a TV detective in the '80s series *Miami Vice*. This no-budget horror film had as its central theme the twin evils of syphilis and gonorrhoea.

Ignoring the clearly marked 18 certificate notification on the movie posters, the boys sauntered to the kiosk, placed a five pound note on the desk and asked for two tickets. Before the cashier could even consider the request, two burly men wearing dark suits and bow ties approached and looked at the two skinny teenagers briefly before telling them that the double bill was for adults only. Bale protested that they were both 18 and stood his ground. The temperature rose as the doormen stated politely but firmly that the two friends were being denied admission for being under age. Bale ignored them and once again demanded a pair of tickets from the cashier. The doormen had seen and heard enough, and the taller of the two men placed his hand on Bale's shoulder.

'Get your fucking hand off me,' the teenager shouted, squaring up to the bouncer. The confrontation ended seconds later as Lorcan Bale was manhandled out the main door and on to the pavement, with Lorcan Conroy following him out.

It was around this time, November 1972, that Lorcan Bale started becoming more serious about his interest in the occult. It is likely that his awareness had developed over a longer period, but in the rigid Catholic environment where the boy was raised and educated, it would have been inappropriate to show such a radical religious deviation from the norm. But Bale's sense of that boundary was eroding.

Bale was never a conventional dresser; perhaps he decided that if he could not fit in, he might as well make an effort to stand out. One day he arrived at school wearing what appeared at first glance to be a shell necklace. This would have been unusual for an Irish '70s schoolboy – jewellery of any type would brand a boy as being effeminate, which was an even more certain guarantee of schoolyard torment than a lack of sportiness. But Lorcan Bale was more than happy to show off his neckwear. It turned out that what looked like shells were actually tiny rat skulls, which he had strung together with strong fishing line. In response to the question of where he managed to find so many rat skulls, he replied that he had set traps in his back garden and then killed the rats before burying them in a lime pit that he had created for this very purpose. Some weeks later the rodents would be fully decomposed leaving skeletons that Bale would then clean, polish and prepare.

In Café Borza on that Friday lunchtime, Lorcan Conroy quizzed him further about the necklace. There, for the first time, Bale revealed that he was a satanist, a way of life that he described as an alternative religion. As for the choker, this, he said, was a satanic alternative to a crucifix. Conroy thought the whole matter absurd, and that his friend was attention seeking. He scoffed at Bale, but not so loudly as to risk provoking his temper.

Like many teenagers, the two Lorcans battled with adolescent spots, not helped by the fact that both were now shaving every day. So when, a few weeks after the necklace event, Lorcan Bale arrived in school with many small marks on his face, Conroy assumed that he had cut himself shaving with a blunt razor. However Bale confided to his friend that he had tried to catch a cat and kill it, but that it had struggled, scratching him badly, and had managed to escape. Later Lorcan Conroy would tell police that Bale had also admitted to killing a neighbour's dog by tying it by the neck to a lamppost and forcing it to, futilely, run.

Despite his initial dismissal, Conroy was curious about Bale's interest in the occult, and it wasn't long until he decided he simply had to find out more. Taking the number 25 bus home from school towards Lucan and Palmerstown, the two sat on the top deck smoking, each lost in their own thoughts. Conroy broached the subject from a distance, but Bale deflected the approach. They fell silent again. Nearing Palmerstown, Bale spoke, revealing that he had joined a secret society, whose activities were by their very nature confidential. Nonetheless, under further questioning, he appeared willing to tease his friend with just a few juicy details.

The society, he whispered, were adults who met on a weekly basis to perform certain rituals. He described the two leaders of the group as a high priest and high priestess, and said that they performed rituals, that there was nudity, and even ritual sex. More than simple sexual gratification, Bale added that the worship of Satan would allow the devotee to achieve success in the material world, success that included the passing of school exams – a skill that appeared to elude both boys. Bale claimed the group were followers of American writer Anton LaVey, author of *The Satanic Bible* and founder of the '60s cult, the Church of Satan. We have no way of knowing whether this was a bizarre attention-seeking fantasy for Lorcan Bale – in his own mind a form of twisted teenage rebellion – or whether such a group actually existed. Certainly Lorcan Conroy was riveted, even if he was unsure whether his friend was being entirely truthful.

In mid-December 1972, an event occurred which suggests strongly that Lorcan Bale may have come into actual contact with adults practicing the occult. Without warning, he disappeared from home for four days. There is no record of where he went, or indeed of the concern his family must have had for his welfare. Later Mr Bale would reveal, 'He went missing from home for a few days before Christmas. And he never gave any real explanation why he did it, except to say he was in County Meath.' A county to the north of Dublin, Meath has a number of highly prized archaeological sites, of great spiritual significance to those with an interest in Ireland's mysterious Celtic heritage. The Hill of Tara, built over 4,000 years ago, is said to be the ceremonial seat of the High Kings of Ireland. Around 430 AD the patron saint of Ireland, Saint Patrick, on his mission to bring the message of Christianity to this land, is said to have visited Tara after setting a symbolic fire on the nearby Hill of Slane. But a more likely journey for Lorcan Bale is to Newgrange, a passage tomb of great historical importance, built over 5,000 years ago, making it older than both Stonehenge and the pyramids at Giza. A remarkable sight and testament to the skill of Neolithic stone-age architecture, the mound has within its roof an ingenious built-in clock, a tiny opening that for just 17 minutes at dawn on the shortest day of the year allows a fine beam of light to penetrate the chamber. With the rising of the sun, the beam then broadens until the entire underground chamber is bathed in bright winter sunshine.

Today modern Druids – gentle, nature-loving pagans who would oppose satanism in all its forms – assemble each year at this UNESCO World Heritage Site to celebrate the winter solstice. It is very possible that Lorcan Bale and his collection of so called satanic friends may also have visited Newgrange around this time, perhaps to conduct a ritual of their own? Certainly the date of the winter solstice – 21 December – is consistent with Lorcan Bale's mysterious disappearance, though hardly conclusive proof that he attended such an event.

After Christmas the two students continued their schooling with limited academic success. Lorcan Bale spoke to his small circle of friends about the joys of meditation, a benign relaxation technique, which today would not warrant further comment. But to his classmates this would have been viewed as an exotic foreign practice, something brought to their notice by the Beatles, who a few short years previously had been devotees of Indian Guru Maharishi Mahesh Yogi. To add further spice to his revelation, Bale stated that to reach the astral plane, meditation should be conducted facing a solitary candle while in the nude. It is doubtful whether any of the company would have known much about the astral plane, mantras, mind projection or indeed yogic flying, but this was one more character trait that set the teenager apart from his peers.

A few weeks later Lorcan Bale brought a shiny silver chalice into Coláiste Mhuire. Had any of the Christian Brothers at this staunchly Catholic school discovered this, he would have been punished, perhaps even expelled. This he surely knew, but the teenager was deeply proud of his latest acquisition; certainly no one would have believed he owned such a thing without seeing it for themselves. Where would a country boy come across a chalice?

Indeed, Bale refused to say how and where he had acquired it, but one can safely assume that this was the very same cup that would be found in the attic on the night of the murder.

Lorcan Conroy remained curious, and would often prod Bale for details of the satanic group he claimed to have joined, most especially the practices at their rites. It was not that he had any interest whatsoever in the occult, but the notion of wild orgies with wicked, nubile high priestesses had filled him with predictable and at times uncontrollable teenage lust. In his own mind he had much to offer the young women of Dublin, yet for reasons that he could not fathom, the opportunity of achieving this goal of real sex with a real girl was still eluding him. A chance to move one step closer to Bale's mysterious occult group came in early 1973 when Lorcan Bale met Conroy's increasing demands to know more about the sect with the suggestion that the two boys conduct a séance. This both intrigued and frightened Conroy, whose knowledge of the occult was confined to vague but dire warnings from the pulpit at Sunday Mass. Deep down he knew it was a bad idea, that he could potentially be playing with fire that was beyond his ability to control. But curiosity got the better of him, in his own mind he was only dabbling, and he agreed to visit the Bale house in Hollyville, Palmerstown, the following Saturday afternoon.

Stepping off the bus that day, Lorcan Conroy found his friend waiting for him. They shared a cigarette and strolled towards number seven, casual as any two boys with nothing planned for the day but an afternoon reading comic books and listening to music. Mrs Bale greeted them in Irish, the language of the house, and beckoned the pair into the kitchen. The three of them made polite conversation, Conroy more than capable of holding his own in Irish after nearly ten years of total immersion in the tongue at Coláiste Mhuire. Lorcan Bale's 14-year-old sister, Anna, was seated in an armchair, lost in a book and ignoring the new arrivals. She had absolutely no idea how attractive their visitor found her to be. Another boy, looking about 12, announced that he was going out to the back field to play football. Putting aside the strange behaviour of the eldest son, it appeared to be a completely and utterly normal household.

Lorcan Bale's bedroom was unexpectedly tidy. It was a bright room facing the main road. He shared it with his little brother, and much of the space was taken up with twin beds. There was also a record player, neatly stacked albums and singles, a few school books, and a laundry basket. To the casual visitor this was a typical teenage boy's bedroom, but it had one unique feature. Bale opened the wardrobe door and pushed back the clothes hanging on the silver rail. He appeared to reach up, as if to make some adjustment to the inner workings of the wardrobe, before inviting his classmate to step forward. Looking up, Lorcan Conroy could see a hole, barely wide enough to admit a skinny teenage boy, that had been carefully crafted into the top of the wardrobe, and, directly above it, an opening of matching size in the ceiling. Hoisting himself up using the shelves within the wardrobe as support, Lorcan Conroy slid through the tiny space into the attic above. Moments later his friend joined him and replaced the trapdoor cover. For a few seconds they were in total darkness, a spell broken as Bale struck a match and used it to light a pair of red candles.

As Lorcan Conroy's eyes adjusted to the candlelight, he surveyed the space around him. To his right were piled boxes, old furniture and stacks of books, the kind of dusty junk found in every attic, no different to what he might have seen in his own, save perhaps for the hammock that had been strung between two rafters. But to the left an area had been cleared and at its centre was what can only be described as a makeshift altar. Constructed from a wooden board neatly covered by a white tablecloth, in the foreground was the same silver chalice that Bale had brought to school weeks before. On either side were small saucers containing unidentifiable white and black powders; there were two playing cards of a type that was unfamiliar to Conroy, and more candlesticks placed at the rear of the rostrum. Directly in front was a wooden

Ouija board, a mysterious object that the visitor had heard many strange tales about, but which he had never before seen.

Most people have heard of Ouija, though few have ever tried it. It's a word with dark and somewhat frightening connections to the supernatural and the demonic. Ouija boards became infamous in the '60s and '70s, popularised immensely by the explosion in the number of horror and witchcraft-themed films made at that time. However, the myth of the board as an ancient device, many centuries or millennia old with its origins and workings lost in the mists of time, is untrue. Though most cultures and civilisations throughout history have attempted to invoke or communicate with spirits or elemental forces, the method of attempting to do so with an Ouija board is thoroughly modern – barely more than 100 years old.

The '70s were not the first time in recent history that people have been interested in the paranormal. The Victorians, despite living in an age of rapid scientific and technological advancement – or perhaps because of this – were captivated by the supernatural. The Victorians gave us *Dracula* and much gothic literature; they were fascinated by ghosts and fairies, and towards the end of the nineteenth century a real craze grew up around the concept of 'mediums' – of people who could commune directly with spirits. Unfortunately it was not as simple as calling up a spirit and asking it to speak; the role of the medium was to act as interpreter. One method was 'table tapping', where participants would place their hands on a table and try to contact a spirit that would manifest itself by thumping or knocking on the table. At the more extreme end of that scale is 'table turning', where the whole table rotates or levitates. The problem with this method was that while it could be dramatic, it was difficult to glean any form of useful message. Even alphabetic table-tapping interpretations could soon become drawn-out, tedious exercises in sentence decoding, and exactly what happens when a spirit is not fluent in English or not able to write is unclear. So towards the end of the nineteenth century, spiritualists started to use boards, which were marked with words or letters. They were known at the time as 'talking boards' or 'spirit boards' – though years later they would be almost universally known as 'Ouija boards'.

The talking board is basically a flat piece of wood – or these days more likely card – with some sort of meaningful symbols inscribed on it. There were many different versions, but the one we know today as the Ouija board started off as a patented spirit board, with a particular arrangement of numbers, letters and words drawn on it. You need a device to single out or point to the letters: in Ouija boards a wedge-shaped piece of wood known as the planchette serves this function. It sits on top of the board, and the users hold it between them, resting their fingers lightly on it. Supposedly, if the séance is successful, the spirit communicates by moving the planchette and spelling out a message. The sceptical argue that minute movements of the hands and fingers are actually responsible. But in any case, the ease of use and increased ability to receive messages of significance helped make spirit boards immensely popular. Séances were increasingly conducted using them.

The board design we know today as the famous Ouija board was in fact only one of many in circulation at the time. That specific design may have been an improvement on the others, however, as its inventors, Charles Kennard and Elijah Bond, went to the trouble of patenting it in 1891. Shortly after filing the patent Kennard found himself ousted and one of his own employees, William Fuld, was installed in his place as company director. Fuld is the name most commonly associated with Ouija. In 1901 he set out to rebrand his company's spirit board, which included giving it the catchy and unique name of 'Ouija board'. He was excellent at promotion, popularising a somewhat sensationalised history of the Ouija board, even claiming that its odd-sounding name had been revealed to Kennard during a séance. Many years on, his various claims have become part of the myths surrounding the Ouija board. Still, at this time and for many years to come, visiting a medium and communicating with spirits was considered exciting and mysterious, but not dangerous, though ironically enough one of the greatest boosts to the popularity of Fuld's Ouija boards was after the man himself died unexpectedly – falling from the roof of his factory as he supervised the replacement of a flagpole. It was a bizarre and strange way to die, and there were those who thought he had jumped – either of his own volition, or under the influence of spirits unknown.

Today the patent for the Ouija board is held by the company Parker Brothers – a North American toy and game producer who make some of the best-known board games in the world, games like Scrabble, Monopoly and Cluedo. Contemporary users are somewhat scathing about the modern mass-produced Ouija board. The glow-in-the-dark letters are seen by some as perhaps a little tacky.

There was religious objection to the Ouija board – indeed, to the very concept of trying to communicate with the dead – from the beginning. The spiritualists were interested in contacting spirits, or ghosts, but the God-fearing were much more concerned about the influence of darker powers. Ouija was seen as opening the user to the influence of evil spirits or even demons and was hideously dangerous because of that. This attitude was greatly reinforced by Hollywood in the '60s and '70s, and even now many who wouldn't describe themselves as religious are wary of Ouija boards. Conversely, for a teen curious about witchcraft, satanism and the paranormal, an Ouija board is an exciting and powerful tool. There is no doubt that Lorcan Bale was proud of his acquisition, though Lorcan Conroy was rather warier.

Sitting down was awkward. Attic flooring is not usually designed to take the weight of a person, making it necessary to place your feet carefully on areas of the most resistance, or to keep entirely to the wooden beams that stretch the length of the attic. Finding a halfway comfortable spot, the two boys sat opposite each other on supporting rafters, the board laid out between them.

'We should really be doing this naked,' whispered Lorcan Bale. A look of panic swept across Conroy's face. He had come to this with reservations, a sensible voice at the back of his mind telling him the séance was a bad idea, and with these first words Bale seemed to have confirmed all his fears. Mute with mortification, Conroy scrambled desperately for some reply. In a well-thumbed copy of *Health & Efficiency* magazine he had read about strange people called 'naturists' who would gather naked and shameless in exclusive German resorts, where they would play undignified games of volleyball. The publication even had photos – somehow slipped past the censor – of busty Scandinavian beauties, whipping off their clothes without a care in the world, relaxing together without embarrassment in steamy saunas before heading out for a bracing dip in an icy lake. But it was one thing to read about, another to do: this boy was Irish, an Irish teenager, a spotty, skinny Irish teenager, who believed firmly that nakedness should be strictly confined to the bath.

Lorcan Bale sensed his friend's discomfort, and to Conroy's profound relief, offered a smile of reassurance and suggested that on this occasion the séance could proceed while fully clothed. Their target in the afterlife was to be a recently deceased child named Tom, who Bale stated was somehow trapped between this world and the next. To contact Tom, all they had to do was empty their minds of all outside thoughts and simply repeat silently the lost young boy's name in the hope that they might draw him in. It sounded very simple.

They closed their eyes and placed their hands, fingers almost touching, just inches above the board. Conroy reached out into the darkest corners of his mind, the hiding place of a person's earliest memories and the repose of those guilty secrets that are best forgotten.

'Tom, I'm calling you,' he repeated to himself over and over again. So far as he could tell, the call went unanswered; he felt not a hint of a foreign presence, nothing. The silence was broken by a groan, a low growling sound, more animal than human. Conroy's eyelids shot open, his heart beating wildly in his chest. What he witnessed was the most frightening scene of his young life: before him, Lorcan Bale was slumped forward, his hands outstretched above the board, with his head facing forward, mouth rasping in a low hiss. Bale's deep blue eyes were wide open, but unblinking, cold and somehow empty. He didn't look human. Conroy couldn't stop himself from crying out, more scared than he could ever remember being, but the noise seemed to break the spell, and the blankness left Bale's eyes. As he sat up, he smiled. The séance had been successful, he said; they had managed to make communication with the lost boy. His classmate, nerves still jangling, decided then and there that he wanted nothing more to do with this creepy foray into the spirit world. He stood up, backing away from the board.

But there was one more earthly revelation in the roof space of number seven that afternoon. Lorcan Bale moved to a corner of the attic, and lay prone on a sheet of plywood placed over a pair of rafters. At the corner of the piece of wood was a tiny hole, no bigger than the nail of his index finger. He peered down the hole from where a small sliver of light was penetrating the darkness. He beckoned Conroy to also take a look; he too lay on his stomach and looked through the spy hole. To his great surprise and wonder, the hole offered a view of part of the Bales' bathroom; more than that, barely three feet from the teenagers was Lorcan Bale's sister, running a bath. Conroy's heart, just beginning to settle after the trauma of the séance, began to quicken once again. He had, for over a year now, indulged in nightly dreams of what it might be like to see the naked form of a girl his age, but the reality, almost in touching distance, far outshone his adolescent fantasy. Transfixed, he watched her undress, the young voyeur surveying every inch of her developing young body. As she climbed into the bath, Bale tugged at the boy's ankle, signalling to him that the viewing was over.

In the field outside, as the two boys shared a cigarette, Lorcan Conroy considered the events of that Saturday afternoon. He had in his own mind sinned twice that day. Between the séance and the unexpected floor show, the 15 year old felt increasingly uneasy.

While not a young man to be racked by religious guilt, he was aware that many of the actions his friend – and he – were engaged in had gone beyond mischief or wickedness, into more serious areas of trespass and wrong. Many teenagers like to rebel against authority, Conroy certainly among them, but he was not without his own moral compass, and he was bothered by some of the things he now found himself doing. As they left the house, he could not help but think that his friendship with Lorcan Bale was leading him down a shady path.

The back field, as it was known, the de facto playground for the children of Hollyville, had one section that was flat enough to serve as a makeshift football pitch, but there were also hidden corners where a boy could play or explore or just sit lost in his own thoughts. Hollyville formed a strong community and the back field was considered by all to be a safe place where neighbour kept an eye on neighbour. Yet in only a few weeks it would become a crime scene, for it was in this field that seven-year-old John Horgan's life would be so cruelly cut short. On this day, the young killer-to-be was pleased to have an audience, someone to share his hobbies with – in this case, his curiosity about animal skeletons. Leading Lorcan Conroy to a point in the field beneath an overhanging ash tree, Bale stopped at a patch of ground, about a foot square, covered in leaves. Carefully removing the dry foliage, the ground beneath was revealed to be completely white. This, he explained, was his lime pit. Refusing to dig into the powder for fear of disturbing the process of decomposition below the surface, Bale outlined in a matter-of-fact way how he would catch rats in traps and then bury them in the pit. In only a few weeks the lime would strip the flesh from the tiny carcasses, leaving nothing but gleaming skeletons.

Conroy was not particularly impressed and moments later the boys began to argue. It is not clear what sparked the row – it may have been connected with the lime pit, or something else. The substance of the argument is of little importance, what matters more is how it escalated. They had brawled before in the school playground, but this was different. While both boys were relatively small and thin for their age, Lorcan Bale was without doubt the stronger of the two. Finger-poking on the chest lead to shoving, and moments later Conroy found himself on his back being pinned to the ground. He tried to twist, to break Bale's hold, to land a blow of his own, but he failed; the other boy was too strong. Leaning against Conroy's chest, Bale pushed his forearm hard against his opponent's throat and began to press down with all his weight. Conroy was powerless to strike back, unable even to break free, and now was struggling to breathe.

He tore at the grass and thumped the ground with his free hand in a desperate effort to signal submission, to communicate to his adversary that he was choking. Today, nearly 40 years later, Lorcan Conroy recalls very clearly the moment when he believed that he was going to die, that his friend was going to kill him.

> I had gone beyond the point of being able to fight back, so was completely at his mercy. I was asthmatic anyway which didn't help, and very quickly I felt myself beginning to black out.
>
> The last thing I remember was looking at Lorcan and his eyes were similar to the way they were at the séance. It was as if he was another person, someone who was closed to any form of communication. I was resigned to death, and I had come to the point where I didn't care whether I lived or died.

The attack ended as quickly as it began. The pressure eased and an instant later reflex had Conroy gulping huge breaths of air into his starved lungs. The waves of blackness that had assailed him lessened, faded and slowly morphed into a wondrous blue sky. Still on the ground, he looked around, seeking out Bale, needing to make sure that the assault was at an end. It was, and his assailant was already half way across the field, strolling in the direction of his home. Lorcan Conroy gingerly picked himself up and headed towards the gate that led to the bus stop. There would be no goodbyes that day. He felt lucky to be alive and was not staying in this place for a minute longer.

Their friendship might have ended that day, but for the fact that as best friends they had been through so much together. There was also the fact that they shared a desk at school, so separation was really not an option. In any event Lorcan Bale had a small number of other friends, including the three elder Browne brothers.

The brothers all attended Coláiste Mhuire and so they often shared bus journeys to the city with Bale. Living near the River Liffey, they would sometimes go fishing for trout, and occasionally met with some success. The youngest of these three elder brothers, Jimmy, recalls that even when fishing, Lorcan Bale's behaviour was disturbing.

> Every time he would catch a fish he would crush it, perhaps with a stone or against a wall. He did the same to frogs. I knew by that stage that he was killing rabbits and pigeons. Cats were going missing too and I'd heard he'd also strangled a dog. But the worst was the rabbits. A guy called Ronnie Dunne would sell us them for pennies. We called them 'Dunne's bunnies', but they never lasted long.

Jimmy, now in his early 50s and living abroad, recalls vividly a night around this time, an evening when his father – who was supplementing his wages working as an entertainer at a local hotel – and mother were both out for the night. The teenager was tasked with babysitting for his younger brothers, a job he had done many times before. With his parents away, the doorbell rang. It was Lorcan Bale. After he left about an hour later, Jimmy Browne realised that all the crucifixes in the house – and there were many – had been turned upside down. With his brothers asleep and feeling somewhat unsettled, he went to bed. Unknown to him, earlier that evening an unseen hand had mixed talc with clear, luminous paint and painted footprints onto the wooden floor of his bedroom. These continued to the wall, the footprints appearing to climb to the ceiling, where, above the boy's bed, was painted a large pentagram. Being luminous paint, Jimmy was blissfully unaware of this artwork until it revealed itself the moment he switched off his bedroom light.

At that exact moment, Jimmy lost the plot. He was so shaken his parents had to come home early. A few days later a priest came to bless the house in a ceremony designed to remove any residual evil.

In 1973, spring gave way to summer, and with summer came the Intermediate Certificate exams. This was the first big test in an Irish student's secondary education. Usually taken around the age of 15, pupils were tested on anything up to 10 subjects, very occasionally more, and could achieve grades from A to E. Today in Ireland, the Intermediate Certificate – better known as the Inter Cert – has been replaced by the Junior Certificate, a broad-based curricular test of a student's acquired knowledge and analytical skills. In the mock exams at Easter, both the Lorcans at Coláiste Mhuire had produced poor results, Lorcan Bale being the academically weaker of the two. In their own different ways, they were under pressure at home to achieve academic success, but by this time it would have required something in the order of divine intervention for them to achieve the results they might have wished for.

The first day of the Inter Cert was a newsworthy event, given the fact that thousands of pupils from all over the country would sit the same exam at the same time. It even warranted a photo spread in the Irish national daily, the *Irish Independent*, who sent a photographer to a nearby school to commit to film the image of a few of Ireland's bright young minds as they wrote their first Inter Cert essays. The photographer Donal Doherty chose Coláiste Mhuire for this assignment and the half-page spread the next morning pictured four boys under the heading 'Exam Day'. One boy looked deep in thought, another was seen writing studiously with a Parker pen; the third photo was of Lorcan

Conroy, writing left-handed with his other hand running through his hair. And on the bottom right of the page was Lorcan Bale, wearing a neatly pressed shirt, writing feverishly.

Thursday 14 June was the fourth day of the Inter Cert exams. At 9.30 a.m. thousands of Irish teenagers – including Bale and Conroy – turned over their geography papers and began writing. Two hours later their time was up. That afternoon's exam was home economics, not a subject typically taken by boys, so Bale and Conroy were free agents as they boarded the number 25 bus for the journey to Palmerstown and Lucan. Conroy remembers that Bale appeared agitated on the journey, as though guarding a secret that he wanted to reveal but dared not. As the bus took the right turn into Palmerstown village, Bale gathered his schoolbag, preparing to ring the bell to alert the driver that his was the next stop. Standing on the upper deck, he held the string used to strike the bell and turned to Lorcan Conroy. Without expressing any great emotion, Bale told his friend that he was due to babysit that day, and that later that afternoon he was going to kill the young boy next door as part of a satanic sacrifice – one that would ensure he would pass his remaining exams. Conroy, by now used to Bale's wild boasts and increasingly bizarre statements, dismissed his words with a shake of his head, telling his friend not to be so stupid. This brief exchange, which appeared so meaningless to him at the time, has haunted Lorcan Conroy for almost four decades.

The die had been cast. Lorcan Bale rang the bell, stepped off the bus and sauntered towards his home.

The two Lorcans would never meet again.

# Four

## The Shrine

Drawing together all the materials for this book has taken many months of research. With virtually nothing reported about the murder in newspapers from the time, it has been on occasion a tortuous journey. I have relied on long-forgotten documents and reports uncovered from dusty archives; also interviews with witnesses, professional experts and people familiar with the victim, the murderer and their families. Collating these statements has required much fact checking to iron out conflicting evidence from witnesses. The passage of time can play tricks with the mind and sometimes when I was satisfied I had a particular sequence of events in the right order, telling the correct details of a particular day, another witness would come out of the woodwork only to shed new and conflicting light on the subject.

When I was giving the finishing touches to this book, my publisher, Bill Campbell from Mainstream Publishing, phoned to say he had received a call from a Garda police officer who was one of the first on the scene on the day of the murder, and that this man was anxious to talk. His name was John O'Loughlin, a native of County Clare, known to friends by his Irish name, Seán. He was enjoying a busy retirement, preparing to jet off the next day to the battlefield site of Gallipoli in Turkey because as an amateur historian he had developed a yearning to learn more of the events of the First World War. Not long after we spoke it became clear that John O'Loughlin was one of the very first officers to respond

97

to the call stating that the Horgan boy was missing, and also that the events of that summer's evening have remained with him all of his life.

Like his superior officer, Detective Sergeant Jim Noonan, O'Loughlin was precise in his recall and meticulous in his choice of words. In a soft rural Irish accent, he remembered,

> On arrival I was met by Mr Horgan, who was in a very agitated state. Initially I presumed this to be a case of a little boy who had wandered off and would soon turn up unharmed. But I was very taken aback when Mr Horgan said to me, 'I know my son is dead, my worry is will we ever find his body.' His concern seemed to be that he believed the boy's body may have been dumped in the river Liffey that runs deep a short distance away.

This must have been quite a shock for a police officer expecting to take part in a brief hunt for a missing child, a search that he had thought would likely conclude with a happy reunion between the boy and his family. O'Loughlin continued,

> Apparently the Horgan boy was last seen going up to the fields at the rear of houses. So I went next door and spoke to Mr Kenneth Bale, the father of the 16-year-old youth, and asked permission to speak to the teenager. I asked Lorcan Bale where the Horgan boy was. He replied that he had left him in the fields. I put it to him that it was unreasonable to leave a young boy alone in the fields and got a distinct feeling that Lorcan Bale was hiding something. While I was speaking to him Bale glanced upstairs a few times.
>
> I asked Mr Bale if I could have a look in the teenager's room upstairs. The bedroom door was locked. His father said he always kept his bedroom locked. A key was produced and I looked round the room, which at first glance was like a normal boy's room. At one end stood a built-in wardrobe

going to the ceiling. I opened the door and saw that it was bereft of any clothing or contents. On the base of the wardrobe broken plasterboard pieces littered the floor. I looked up and saw a passage had been cut in the ceiling large enough for a person to fit through. I asked Lorcan Bale who had crafted the hole in the ceiling and he said that this was all his own work, that he was responsible.

Garda O'Loughlin went to the patrol car and got a torch. Rather than attempt to enter the attic through the hole in the wardrobe, he decided to use the main entry at the top of the stairs. As there were no steps to the attic the young Garda officer stood on the banister and pushed up the trapdoor.

His voice hesitated slightly as he recalled the scene that awaited him.

I was met with a sight that still haunts me to this day. The naked body of the Horgan boy was lashed to a makeshift cross from the rafters, while in front of him on the ceiling floor was an elaborate altar. I checked carefully for signs of life, but there were none.

Other records of the events of that day differ very slightly in the detail, but the substance of the search and subsequent discovery of the body remains consistent.

A slightly differing version, which I've recounted in detail in Chapter One, is Detective Sergeant Noonan's account, supplemented by other witnesses. It begins at the hour when the sun had almost set on that June evening and tells of Lorcan Bale being confronted outside by Noonan and other officers, and his father. At the threat of the house being searched, Bale offers to show them all to John Horgan's body, confessing, when pressed, that it is in the attic. Noonan, too, remembers the moment of entering the attic and seeing 'something that was neither wall nor furniture – a small, pale shape, the body of seven-year-old John Horgan, naked, arms outstretched, suspended from the rafters'. Noonan, too, says he rushed to find some signs of life.

The discrepancies between the two policemen's accounts can easily be explained by the passage of time. But common to both is seeing the body and immediately checking for any signs of life. Clearly the child was already dead, indeed the autopsy report presented by Professor Maurice Hickey states the exact nature of the trauma to the child's brain, injuries which would likely have killed him instantly.

Soon afterwards, the harrowing news was broken to the Horgan family, and though one can barely imagine the impact this would have had on his frantic parents, those who were there remember that the Horgans faced the devastating news with extraordinary courage and dignity.

Garda O'Loughlin goes further, recalling a reaction of remarkable Christian forgiveness:

> On telling Mr and Mrs Horgan, that I had found the body of their little angel, Mrs Horgan paused, then said that this boy was a gift from God and that the Lord had intended them to have him for seven years only. There was no aggression or talk of revenge, as one would naturally expect under these terrible circumstances.
>
> Later that evening, after the boy's body was taken down and was lying on a couch awaiting removal for post-mortem, a local priest arrived to give the last rites. I asked the cleric where in his opinion all this black magic pointed. The priest gestured to the little corpse, and said, 'That's where it leads to.' I need not have asked.

Outside as dusk was beginning to envelop the area, the civilian searchers received word that the hunt for the boy was to be called off for the night. Local butcher Dessie Cloak spoke for his neighbours when he approached a Garda police officer. Referring to Mrs Horgan, he said, 'We can't leave a woman in this condition looking for her child. There are plenty of men here willing to stay up all night if we have to.'

The officer placed his hand on the butcher's shoulder, looked at him directly in the eye and replied, 'We're acting on information. Go home, have a rest and we'll see you in the morning.' Dessie Cloak was left with the clear impression that the man in uniform knew more than him, and suspected that it was about to emerge that the Horgan boy had fallen victim to some terrible accident, but the notion that the child may have been murdered never for a moment entered his mind.

Minutes later word began to filter through to those gathered outside that the body of young John Horgan had been found in the attic of the Bale house, and that the eldest Bale boy had somehow been involved. Neighbours do not recall the exact reaction of the Bales to learning what one of their own had done, but it is said that they were – understandably – stunned and devastated. Can you still love your son, your brother, after finding out he's a murderer?

Detective Inspector Willie Reynolds joined Detective Sergeant Jim Noonan in the attic as they began to examine the space, now a crime scene, which they would have to officially describe. Child murders in Ireland were at that time mercifully rare – indeed, they still are. But from the first glance, both officers could see that this was no ordinary case. The body had been carefully and ritualistically arranged; the attic was full of strange objects and articles, set out in odd patterns or with no discernible function. Then there was the manner of their teenage suspect – quiet, calm and still. It all pointed to a murder unlike any other in the nation's history. They also had to consider the suspect's age, just 16. If he were tried, it would be as a juvenile, and if convicted, he could not be sent to an adult prison, at least not until he was aged 21. This was uncharted territory. In the history of the modern Irish state, there had never been a case where a child had been murdered by another juvenile.

The two officers first noted the positioning of the body: John's arms had been stretched out to either side, giving his body a cruciform appearance; each wrist had been tied firmly at either side to the long support beam that ran the length of the attic. His legs were loosely bound, and his feet rested gently on the corner of a soft cushion chair seat. Red, nylon clothes-line cord was twined around his body, tied secure under his ribcage, and attached in turn to the support beam, to hold his body upright. Even his head was held up by a light cord that ran under his chin and fastened to a nail above his head. He had been gagged, and wore nothing except for a blue-and-green-striped necktie. His eyes were closed.

Some four feet to the right of the body there was a stand, which looked disturbingly like some sort of altar. It was about two feet tall, consisting of three large wooden boards that had been fitted around a water tank, and the topmost of which supported a bizarre and inexplicable collection of objects. The centrepiece was a silver-plated cup that appeared to be a chalice, with a tall white candle to either side of it and a yellow household duster placed over it. In front of the chalice rested a bowl full of sand. This was encircled by five small candles, evenly spaced, like the points of a pentagram. To the left of the chalice was an alarm clock, either broken or stopped, showing five o'clock, approximately the time of the murder. There was a bronze bell and two tarot cards, 'the devil' and 'the lovers'. The lid of a sweet tin held three tiny bottles, all empty, a mustard jar containing dried petals, a tin box and a piece of black charcoal. There were ten tapers alongside a box of incense cones, and matches. There was a pair of scissors, and a large carving knife.

Everything had clearly been chosen with care and, in the mind of Lorcan Bale, had significance both within his own beliefs and in relation to the murder. The chalice, for example, is the centrepiece of the satanic *black* mass, just as it is the Catholic one. The incense was likely chosen to give a similarly religious tone, though along with the sand it could also have had a more elemental, pagan significance. The pentagram is a well-known symbol, commonly associated with witchcraft – both the dark, satanic kind and the benevolent, benign type. Some of the objects are more mysterious – items like the bronze bell, the flower petals and the stopped clock, all three interesting and almost poetic, but we can only speculate on their significance. Their interpretations are too many and varied for any certainty. What is beyond doubt is that they were all special, religiously, symbolically or magically significant to Lorcan Bale himself.

More detailed, though still uncertain, interpretation can be drawn from the two tarot cards. Like many other aspects of the occult, fortune telling using tarot cards is a broadly understood concept that is nonetheless surrounded by myths and misinformation. Unlike Ouija boards, tarot cards really do have some history, though not perhaps as glamorous a one as some might imagine. They've been around in their modern form since the fourteenth century, when they were originally used as playing cards. Indeed, the minor arcana – the suit cards, divided into cups, wands, pentacles and swords – are more or less the same as those in modern playing cards, except that they have one extra face card and different names for the suits. You could play poker with them quite easily. The better-known tarot cards are the major arcana: that's where cards like 'the tower', 'the world' and 'the hanged man' are found. Despite their light-hearted beginnings, tarot cards are now used almost exclusively in fortune telling and divination. The large number of cards and the various and multilayered meanings ascribed to each allow for extremely varied and specific divinatory messages to be interpreted.

The popular or assumed meanings of some of the cards are often inaccurate. For example, the death card is often dealt to sudden dramatic effect and jolting background music in Hollywood horror movies, but books on the subject and practitioners usually understand it as signifying change – endings and beginnings and a certain amount of chaotic transition. Similarly 'the lovers' are far more metaphorical than literal: the two figures in the card are meant to represent choice. A change, a fork in the road, is approaching, and only one path can be taken. The image used is of a man choosing between two lovers, but the meaning behind it is much broader than one of romantic indecision.

The devil card is similar in tending to generate misinterpretation. It has a couple of different meanings, but neither of these refer to the actual devil, or demons. Some even say that the figure on the card is not the Christian devil at all, but an older God, like Pan or Dionysus. For reasons that are obvious when you look at the card, the most common meaning for it is bonds, or chains, either the forging or the breaking of them. It's a card that's commonly associated with temptation or materialism – though not with pleasure or wealth itself, more with the way they can enslave our minds and set us in habits that become increasingly difficult to break. There is also a second interpretation of the card, to do with the unconscious mind. Many practitioners of divination or magic believe the unconscious to be a well of untapped power, but beyond the ability of most people to access. The devil card can symbolise that unconscious power.

It is possible that Bale's choice of the two cards was meant to symbolise his move to a new path, and a desire either to affirm his links with the darker powers, or to shatter the bonds of human frailty and weakness that he felt held him back. But all interpretation in this case is purely speculation – while we know of some of the books that influenced Bale, we do not know where or how he learned about the Tarot, so although inferences can be drawn from modern commonly accepted meanings of the cards, we do not know if that was Bale's understanding of them.

The objects on the rest of the stand were no less strange. On the ground to the left of it was a biscuit tin containing a table knife, several small marble stones, three wax candles, two artist's painting brushes and a wooden pipe. There was an unmarked glass jar containing a white powder, and a small tin containing black powder, neither of which was obviously identifiable. There was a saucepan, which was found to contain human excreta.

Folded on the attic floor, between the altar and the body, was a strange grey blanket covered with multi-coloured, hand-sewn designs. Two armholes had been cut out of the top, turning the blanket into something that might serve as a crude cloak. Resting on top of it was a red silk vest. The garments sound almost ceremonial; certainly they weren't clothes that could have been worn every day, or outside, they were too strange, and the inexpert design suggests they may have been made or refashioned by Bale himself.

Strewn along the floor between the attic entrance and the body were the remains of the clothes that John Horgan had been wearing: a red jumper and grey trousers, white vest and underpants, all cut open; also blue canvas shoes and a green necktie. In the pocket of the trousers was an empty Cadbury's Aztec chocolate wrapper. Two unopened bars of the same chocolate lay near the body. A large sack sat empty in front of the body, and beside it was a present that had been stolen months earlier from the victim, a boy's Raleigh Chipper bicycle.

In Noonan's account of that evening, as the police checked and catalogued the objects displayed in this disturbing tableau, they found a second entrance to the attic in the far north-eastern corner. This consisted of a hole in the ceiling, which was found to lead to the bedroom of their teenage suspect, Lorcan Bale.

Books were found, both in the attic and in Bale's bedroom, that can give us clues as to what, exactly, was going through his mind. One was *Crime and Punishment*, the heavyweight Russian classic by Fyodor Dostoevsky that follows a very ordinary man who, one day, decides to commit a murder. He chooses his victim carefully and dislikes her enough that he has no expectation of being burdened with any remorse. But though he succeeds in his murder, events quickly spiral out of his control and it emerges that things are not going to be quite as simple as he had planned. The murder is interrupted, so he must kill a second woman if he wishes to get away with the murder of the first, and such is his panic that he doesn't even succeed in his original purpose, which was theft of the valuables she owned. As the book goes on, various other characters are introduced, some antagonistic – the police officer who comes to suspect him – and others more sympathetic, their function being to mirror the protagonist, or expand the various consequences. The murderer finds himself increasingly troubled by what he has done, and is eventually driven half mad with guilt and the need to confess. *Crime and Punishment* is considered one of the great works of literature, and though none of the various English translations that exist can be considered perfect, it's still an extremely powerful read, delving deeply into the twists and turns of a mind undergoing profound turmoil. This is an odd, and sad, book for a soon-to-be-murderer to own. Obviously the message about the importance of laws, in a moral sense, and the consequences of murder – for the murderer, as much as anyone else – did not make much of an impact on Bale.

Another book was the infamous *Confessions of Aleister Crowley*, which he may have found more to his taste. This very long and very strange book reads like a combination of bizarre world-travel tales with a how-to guide to mysticism, with a bit of sex magic for spice. To a bored, rebellious teenage boy with an interest in the occult, it would truly have been required reading. A man of enormous ego and equally sizeable character, Crowley was born in Warwickshire, Britain, in 1875, to a family who were extremely religious. He started to lose his faith after the death of his father, and by the time he was at university he was a thorough sceptic. He became interested in mysticism and the occult and spent some time as a member of the Hermetic Order of the Golden Dawn, a semi-secret society with an interest in magic and spiritual development, but left a few years later over differences in philosophy. He joined other mystical orders, investigated various eastern philosophies including yoga, and travelled widely. He lived a bohemian, hedonistic life, and when it came to sex and drugs his attitudes were less Victorian gentleman and more '60s rock-and-roll star. Perhaps in his own most peculiar way, Crowley was ahead of his time.

Crowley would probably not have described himself as a satanist, but he certainly shares many of the traits of those who do: an utter fixation on his personal power and personal pleasures, among them, and a rejection of religion that was so strong it seemed to require an equally strong and equally all-encompassing belief system to replace it. His notes on magic are long, detailed and comprehensive and he spent his life searching assiduously for new understanding and secrets of the occult.

The other books that were found in the attic were about magic too, though they were more instructive and less biographical, in a far more typical satanic style. It was likely here that Bale developed his ideas about rituals and magic. One of the books, *Mastering Witchcraft* by Paul Hudson, even has instructions for forming a coven. There is some evidence that Bale tried to interest others in the occult, and it's possible that a group like a coven might have been a wish of his.

We cannot truly know what was going through the mind of Lorcan Bale as he planned the murder of John Horgan, as he carried it out and invoked his bizarre ritual. We cannot know if he truly expected it to work. It does seem clear that although he thought a great deal about what he was going to do, he didn't give a lot of consideration to *afterwards*. Perhaps he thought his new powers would make the issue moot. Under questioning, it emerged that Lorcan Bale believed he had the power to communicate with his victim. But he crumbled quickly when interviewed by police, and only a handful of hours after the murder, he had been accused, arrested and charged.

So, at 11.30 p.m. that evening, Lorcan Bale was sitting in a squad car, accompanied by his father and three police officers, driving to the local Garda police station in Lucan. On arrival he was given the standard police caution, which the teenager confirmed that he understood. And it was in the sergeant's office, in the presence of three officers and his father, that Lorcan Bale in a very matter-of-fact way confessed to the murder of John Horgan.

His confession shows no sign of regret or grief; its tone would not look out of place if put against the confession of a young thief caught stealing a crate of beer from a local corner store. Yet as the teenager settled down for his first fitful night in custody, he must have realised it would be a very long time indeed before he would ever have control of his own life again. One can't help but wonder if he had really expected to get away with his crime.

While the murder had been solved within hours of it taking place, there was still a great deal to be done before the case could go to court. Detective Sergeant Noonan returned in the small hours of the morning to seven Hollyville where he was met by a police photographer and forensic expert whose tasks would be to examine and document every inch of the scene. In the course of this examination the yellow duster was removed from the top of the silver chalice, and the team found to their dismay that it contained three hosts – circular Communion wafers, the most sacred elements of the Catholic Mass. Within the Roman Catholic tradition, a host that has been consecrated by a priest through the divine act of transubstantiation becomes the actual body of Christ, taken by the faithful in memory of the sacrifice made by Jesus Christ as symbolised in the Last Supper. Neither Noonan nor Reynolds thought it appropriate for these objects to be bagged and tagged with the rest of the evidence, locked away until the day of Lorcan Bale's trial. This unwelcome discovery, they decided, required handling at a higher spiritual level. Fortunately a solution was close at hand, for ministering to the distraught Horgan and Bale families was a Dalkey priest, Father Richard Mulcahy, who was prevailed upon to remove the hosts from the cup.

Today, the notion of a civilian removing material evidence from a crime scene would be deemed absolutely unacceptable, serious enough to spark questions to politicians and an explanation from senior police chiefs. But again I stress how different a country Ireland was in the '70s; the priest was the pillar of society, the abuse scandals that would rock the Catholic Church were still decades away. This particular cleric, Monsignor Richard Mulcahy, was not just a regular parish priest, but the head of Opus Dei in Ireland, a secretive organisation known for its advocacy of traditional Catholic values. A close family friend of the Horgans, Monsignor Mulcahy also formally identified the body as being that of young John Horgan.

The police forensic team worked through the night, meticulously recording every detail of the scene, even though the case had effectively been solved hours before. It was at 4 a.m. that the body of little John Horgan was removed from the attic and given into the care of Kirwin's Undertakers.

Nobody slept that night. For many, it would be many nights yet before sleep came quickly or easily again. It was very early the next morning when Bale was taken from Lucan Garda station to retrace his steps of the previous day. Detective Inspector Willie Reynolds, Detective Sergeant Noonan and Mr Bale accompanied the teenager as he led them to the back field, pointing out the route he had taken less than 24 hours previously. At one point in the reconstruction Lorcan Bale stopped, in a corner of a field near a large hedge. He had intended killing the boy here, he informed the investigators, but had changed his mind when he looked up and realised he would be visible from the upstairs windows of the Hollyville houses. Why did he say this – even if it was correct? Was he trying to be helpful to the investigators? Or was he being arrogant and proud, trying to show off how smart he had been? Perhaps a more likely explanation is that the 16 year old was scared, finally realising the kind of trouble he was in.

With the reconstruction completed, itself the last piece of necessary evidence in the case of the murder of John Horgan, Bale was taken back to Lucan Garda station. There, at a specially convened assembly, Peace Commissioner Mr Harold Lynch charged 'Lorcan Maolmhuire Bale (16) with the murder of John Joseph Horgan (7) on the fourteenth of June 1973'. The hearing lasted only a few minutes. Lorcan Bale was remanded to be held in custody at St Patrick's Institution in Central Dublin, an institute for young offenders that was only a few miles north of his school, with the instruction to appear again before a district judge in Howth Court the following Monday.

The news travelled through Palmerstown like wildfire. Though rumours flew furiously, there was almost no official reporting, and, in the absence of fact, wild and inaccurate stories began to circulate. But they all agreed on three main points: the murder victim was a child, the perpetrator was himself just a teenager, and the whole thing had something to do with the occult. It was this last that inspired the most frenzied of speculation.

The newspaper reporting was starkly lacking. On 15 June the *Irish Independent* printed a black-and-white photo of John Horgan and reported,

> A seven-year-old boy was found dead in a neighbour's attic late last night after a search in Palmerstown, Dublin. The boy, John Horgan, Hollyville, Lucan Road, had been missing since 4 pm. A 14-year-old juvenile was last night helping Gardai with their inquiries, but it is believed the death was accidental.

On the same day, the *Irish Press* also reported that the death appeared to be a tragic accident: 'A 14-year-old youth was being questioned by Gardaí early today but it is believed that the death of the boy, John Horgan, Hollyville, Lucan Road, was accidental.' Both papers reported in error that the teenager being held was aged 14 – he was 16 at the time – however the more serious error, that of not stating the murder for what it was, is much more difficult to explain.

No editor likes to bury a story, and it is very unlikely that this story was suppressed from inside a newspaper office. But when you consider that most stories of this nature begin their life in a police press office, things become clearer. There are several possible explanations for the inaccurate reporting of that day – either the police themselves were in possession of inaccurate and incomplete information, which they passed on to the newspapers in error, or the authorities felt it necessary to withhold certain details in this case. Why would they do this? One can speculate that some of the more unpleasant aspects of the murder, most especially the satanic overtones, were omitted out of a belief that they may have caused some kind of moral panic. There is no direct documentary evidence of any suppression, but the published inaccuracies of the newspapers that day beg the question. It was hardly without precedent: in the '70s there were several areas of moral depravity that were prevalent in Ireland, but were barely reported at all. Clerical sex abuse, physical abuse at industrial schools, infanticide, banishment of 'fallen' women to work in laundries – all were practices now seen as scandalous and horrific, but they were barely discussed at the time. So could it be that a satanic murder was also considered a topic best left unspoken? There is no direct evidence of any suppression, but the published inaccuracies of the newspapers that day beg the question.

The coming days brought no more facts to light. Once Lorcan Bale was charged, the case would be considered *sub judice*, so nothing could from that moment be reported which might be seen to prejudice the trial. In addition, because Bale was in the eyes of the law a juvenile at the time of the trial, his age but not his name could be published in the newspapers. If the public were waiting to find out the true facts of the case at the trial, they were to be disappointed.

The rumours that spread across west Dublin became ever more lurid and fanciful. 'Crucified' was a word commonly used to describe the murder, though given the fact that John is understood to have died instantly following a blow to the back of his head in the field behind Hollyville, this is technically inaccurate. Clearly, however, the way Bale chose to pose the body after death was a deliberate imitation of the crucifixion, so this rumour had some currency. Some stories even referred to the boy having been 'crucified upside down', but witnesses state that this is simply not the case.

There was also widespread speculation that Coláiste Mhuire

had within it a secret satanic society. This, too, was nonsense, but the few boys who had been close to Bale in school, including Lorcan Conroy, found they were shunned by schoolmates. Another source claimed that in Lucan Garda Station, when questioned after the murder, Lorcan Bale was heard repeatedly shouting the words 'O Master, I have failed you! O Master, I have failed you!' and crying out that he had to find another victim, a young girl, a virgin to be sacrificed. Again, there is no evidence whatsoever to back this up, so it should be dismissed, along with most of the other speculation.

On the morning of Saturday 17 June, Mr and Mrs Horgan met with a local priest at their home, number six Hollyville, to prepare for the funeral of their son John Horgan. Prayers were said in the home prior to the funeral Mass at St Philomena's. In what was a remarkable act of compassion and forgiveness, the Horgans reached out to the distraught Mr Bale on that day and asked him to share in their prayers for the soul of the lost boy. Though the circumstances were very different, perhaps there is a loose comparison to be made with Gordon Wilson, a man who 15 years later, in 1987, would lose his daughter in the Remembrance Sunday bombing in Enniskillen, Northern Ireland. As father and daughter lay under the rubble, Gordon Wilson found the courage to join together the twin powers of pain and love, forgiving those who stole his daughter's life. Many believe that his courage to forgive allowed good to triumph over the evil of the Poppy Day bombing. Indeed today many people remember the Enniskillen bomb more for Gordon Wilson's remarkable compassion than for the outrage of the attack itself.

In Palmerstown local residents pondered whether to go to John Horgan's funeral that Saturday morning. One parishioner stated, 'We didn't know what to do. We wanted to show our support to the family, but we were afraid to go. Because of what happened and how it happened we didn't want to appear to be gaping, as the entire community had so much respect for the Horgan family.' But in the end there was a large turnout, including many of the boy's school friends from Mount Sackville. At the foot of the altar of St Philomena's rested a closed white coffin, past which the entire congregation filed respectfully, their heads bowing. The solemnity of the day was marred by a single act of crass immaturity from a local teenager, a troublesome boy of the type that Hollyville folk would have preferred lived somewhere else. On reaching the top of the queue, the boy stood next to the coffin, then knocked loudly at its timbers before offering a two-handed thumbs up to the congregation. The elders were rightly outraged and seconds later the teenager was bundled out the church door. After the funeral Mass, the body of John Horgan was taken to Balgriffin Cemetery in north County Dublin where, in a private ceremony, he was laid to rest in the family plot.

From late summer 1973, mothers in Palmerstown began to warn their children that Lorcan Bale had a list with anything up to a dozen names on it – names of fresh-faced, blond, young boys who he *and his accomplices* might sacrifice. With no list found in the attic and all the evidence pointing to Bale having acted alone, early on I dismissed the notion of 'Lorcan's list'. Yet witnesses kept referring to it: two, three, five, seven people, all telling the exact same story. One lifetime Palmerstown resident, Stevie Vincent, a well-grounded television picture editor now in his 40s, approached me stating that he grew up believing he was on Lorcan's list.

Chillingly, it turned out he was right.

About a week after John Horgan's death, Michael Smallwood, one of the boys who Bale had warded off with a rude hand gesture after the murder, was once again in the back field pondering the terrible events of the previous days. He stopped at a large rat hole and, for no particular reason other than boredom, began poking a stick into it. To his surprise the end of the twig snagged something, a length of string. Michael pulled on the cord until, from deep within the burrow, a small canvas bag emerged. Curious as to its contents, he opened it.

Inside were some torn pages from occult magazines, a couple

of curious artefacts that the boy did not recognise and, at the bottom of the bag, a small notebook. Michael gave it to his father who in turn passed it on to the police. There were around ten names listed, including three girls. All lived locally, all had blue eyes and fair hair and all were young children. Everyone in Hollyville knew each person on the list well, including the boy who was no longer among them.

As days passed into weeks that summer, locals in Palmerstown struggled to come to terms with the terrible tragedy that had struck their little village. The one question nobody could answer was 'Why?' Exactly what prompted Lorcan Bale to commit this act? It was too simplistic to dismiss it as evil and therefore beyond rational understanding, and neither could people be satisfied by explanations that absolved Bale of responsibility. Perhaps an easier question to begin with would be: 'Why satanism?'

In some ways the greater puzzle of this sad tale is how Bale ever came into contact with the occult at all. Ireland in the '70s was in so many ways a different place: no high-speed Internet with the freedom of quick, easy, anonymous research on any conceivable topic with no more effort than it takes to press a few keys. The few seconds it takes to search Wikipedia and the minute or two of skimming the resulting article may glean us more information than could be found in weeks of patient searching through bookshops, magazines, libraries and other publications. Moreover, the cultural attitudes were very different. The Church was the moral authority, the unquestioned source of information on right, wrong and how to live your life. You were not expected to deviate from its teachings, or to try to form your own, personal moral code. That would be an act of pride verging on intolerable egotism. Many modern attitudes that we take for granted today – concepts like political correctness and tolerance for alternative lifestyles – were nascent or non-existent. The local library was vanishingly unlikely to have books available on how to practise Ouija, but even if they had, the librarian may well have refused to lend such a book to a young and impressionable teenage boy, and though today such action would be seen as an unacceptable imposition of personal beliefs, in those days the librarian would not have considered it anything but sensible and responsible.

Of course this is not to say that satanism was unheard of – far from it. Even '70s Ireland was not immune from the fascination with the occult that gripped Hollywood in those years. Films like *The Exorcist* (1973) and *Rosemary's Baby* (1968) were two of the most famous of the time and are still scaring audiences today, but huge numbers of lower-budget and lower-profile films were made too. Perhaps it was some sort of reaction to the way science seemed to be explaining everything about the mundane world that drove people to seek mystery in the supernatural one.

With this in mind perhaps we can begin to answer our first question. Satanism was something that you only heard of in grisly, sensationalist films, and what was known of it was correspondingly inaccurate. To a frustrated and angry teen from a devout and religious background, it must have seemed the ultimate form of rebellion. Satanism takes many of its influences from Catholicism, indeed seems at times a deliberate mockery of that particular branch of the Christian faith. However these two apparent opposites do rest on a surprising number of shared assumptions – the existence of the Christian God and the Devil; the power of the Bible, though in the case of satanism the power derives from the Bible being defaced or profaned; many of the same accoutrements are present in both Catholic Masses and satanic masses, like the use of an altar, the use of the ceremonial chalice, the presence of a priest. Even the satanic mass is little more than an inversion of the Christian one. Examined objectively, satanism looks like little more than failed Catholic rebellion, an attempt to lash out at the faith, but not to break away from it entirely. In this context we can see why it might have been attractive to someone like Lorcan Bale, giving a direction and outlet to his desire for mutiny without truly challenging his paradigm.

One thing is certain. Bale did not dream up the ritual of the killing of John Horgan by himself. That he considered himself a satanist we know, but what were the influences that shaped his choices on that day? The books that were found in his room during the course of the police investigation may have shed some light on that question, but the fact remains that a great many people have watched *The Exorcist* (1973) and not tried to summon demons, or seen *Psycho* (1960) and not attempted to murder innocent bathers. While we can analyse and unpick the various threads that may have made up the details of that grisly day, we must not get so caught up in them that we miss the bigger picture. *Did Bale commit murder because he was a satanist?* It is far more likely that he became a satanist in order to justify committing murder, or at least to justify causing harm and pain. The question is not 'What was he interested in?' but 'Why was he interested in this?' How does someone develop the urge to kill? What forces can transform a boy so young into a murderer?

Palmerstown was abuzz with questions concerning the occult, though answers were in short supply. A bizarre postscript to these terrible events came about a week after John Horgan's death when Detective Sergeant Jim Noonan and another detective, Terry Smyth, a colleague from Lucan district, returned to the scene. They felt it important to have a thorough inspection of the area in daylight so that no detail would be missed. Noonan and Smyth were aware of local lore about trees, particularly ash trees, which have been regarded with reverence in Celtic countries for centuries, especially in Ireland. There are a number of documented cases in Irish history in which people refused to cut an ash tree, even when wood was scarce, for fear of having their houses consumed with flame. Water diviners use ash seedpods to find underground streams, and the wood is said to have the power to ward off fairies, as well as protecting against witchcraft. Noonan recalls the day well.

This may sound odd, but I had read that occasionally after a murder, an ash tree within a one-mile radius of the crime scene would be damaged, typically by having its top branches cut off. So sure enough, when Terry Smyth and I were walking through the field behind Hollyville a week or so after the crime, there was one large ash tree that had wood chippings strewn around its base. We both looked up and to our surprise the top branches were missing.

The most likely explanation is that the tree had been struck by lightning – electrical storms are quite common in Ireland in high summer. Nonetheless, the two detectives found the experience quite unnerving.

Also unsettling was an unexpected discovery during my research for this book. Because the murder was largely unreported, I was forced back to what remains the most effective form of journalism – knocking on doors. It is a means of research that can give unexpected results and revealing insights. Finding so little on the Internet or in archives, I drove to Hollyville and began speaking to the residents. Most people in the area had moved there after 1973, so had no firsthand memories of the murder, but for some older folks it was like pressing a button, one that released suppressed memories of an event almost forgotten. The people I met proved to be engaging and hospitable, mostly kind, warm pensioners, but some middle-aged people too. Many made time to talk about an event that had touched their lives.

Not long after the murder, both the Horgans and the Bales had moved away. The Bales had trouble selling their house – perhaps its dark history deterred potential buyers – so for many years it was a rental property. Eventually it was sold, though the present owner was until recently not aware of his home's history. The victim's house was bought by a couple, Ben Lynam and his wife. They had no children and lived happily in Hollyville for the rest of their days. The present owners, Paul and Vera Stewart, were unaware that their home held a secret and were interested – from an historic point of view – to know the full story.

Chatting and sharing a cup of tea one evening, Mrs Stewart, a slender, blonde Dubliner, said that she had something to show me. Her husband filled in the details: some 15 years earlier they had converted their attic to create an extra bedroom. The builders cleared out long forgotten boxes from the roof space, but there was one item they refused to touch. He beckoned me upstairs. The converted roof space was now a big, bright, airy bedroom, some 24 feet long and almost as wide. Mrs Stewart produced a large brown envelope and opened it carefully. Inside was a brass crucifix, clearly very old, about a foot long, and engraved with a number of curious markings. Mr Stewart said that the builders had found it wedged between two supporting joists in the attic; they asked if I knew what type of cross it was, and more importantly why it was there? Looking closely at the crucifix, I could see a skull and bones at the feet of the Christ figure, and on the reverse was what appeared to be an inverted version of the Sacred Heart. I agreed to make enquiries and took the crucifix away with a promise to return it safely.

I showed it to a colleague, a television producer specialising in religious broadcasting, who pointed out that the skull and bones was sometimes used in religious iconography as *memento mori* – reminders of mortality. It may simply have been a pointer to the belief that Jesus was crucified at Golgotha, a place name that translates as 'the place of the skull'. He found the emblem on the reverse to be curious, perhaps a corruption of the Sacred Heart. Where normally the Sacred Heart appears pierced by a lance, the arrow here seemed to be coming from above.

So what did it all mean? Given that a child who lived in the house had been murdered, his body discovered in the attic next door, could the crucifix have been left as a holy gatekeeper, a symbol of good to guard against the evil that had afflicted the area?

The crucifix turned out to be French, from about 1880, but its provenance did not explain its purpose. I have never put great stock in the belief that an earthly object could have divine power, so it was with mixed emotions that I began to investigate the use of a crucifix in ritual ceremonies. The Catholic Church in Dublin does not have an official exorcist, but there are a small number of priests who quietly carry out 'deliverance', ministering to people believed to be demonically possessed. Father Clement Keane is one such priest who agreed to meet on the sole condition that his true name would not be published; he fears that publicity would bring to his door dozens of disturbed people whose need is for a psychiatrist as opposed to a priest. We sat in a small ante room of his church, where he spoke first about his work.

> When I see people looking for manifestations of the diabolical, in most cases there are underlying psychological problems, but I do believe that in a very small number of cases, a malevolent evil can be attached to a person.
>
> I have a case at the moment, a man where in our first session I tried to understand whether his problems were spiritual or psychological. I didn't really know what to think at the end of our session, so I offered to pray for him. The second I spoke, a new voice broke out from the man's mouth, a vulgar highly blasphemous personality, spitting a torrent of abuse that mocked my work. For our next session I was joined by another priest and we ministered together. Again, the mocking derisory voice appeared, but by the end of the session it had shifted. Now three years later the man has returned with the same problem. It can take years to cleanse a person.

He seemed relieved to hear that I was not seeking personal deliverance and carefully examined the crucifix I had brought. After listening to the story behind the cross, where it was found, the tragic death of the Horgan boy and the strange circumstances of the murder, the priest declared, 'It is a perfectly conventional crucifix, though it does have an unusual combination of brass and wood.'

'What is the relevance of wood?' I asked.

'If you were to leave a cross in such circumstances, wood would be the preference,' he said, shifting the crucifix from hand to hand. 'Christ's cross was made of wood so if there were a devil present, he would have more respect for wood. The skull and crossbones refer to Golgotha, the place of death, and the Sacred Heart on the reverse signifies the biblical prediction of the Passion.'

'So how might the crucifix have been used?' I inquired, as he replaced the cross into the brown envelope.

'There may have been a need to re-consecrate the house, to claim it back from a demonic influence.' He paused for a moment. 'Sometimes the spirits of the dead can disturb a place if something traumatic has occurred there in the past, a happening such as abuse, abortion or murder.'

I thanked the priest for his time and returned to the Stewarts' home, the semi-detached house where the cross had hung silently in the attic for decades.

It felt apt to return the crucifix to its rightful place.

# FIVE

## *Penal Servitude for Life*

The day after the killing, Friday 15 June, Peace Commissioner Mr Harold Lynch charged Lorcan Bale with the murder of young John Horgan and then ordered that the prisoner be taken to St Patrick's Institution in Dublin to await his next court hearing. As is normal in such cases, there would be several remand hearings in the months ahead, prior to the full criminal court trial where the accused's guilt or innocence would once and for all be established.

St Patrick's Institution was – and still is – a juvenile prison for young offenders between the ages of 16 and 21. It is located beside Mountjoy Prison, home to some of the country's most notorious adult prisoners. The two institutions are separated by a single high wall. Typically prison staff would not receive a list of . arrivals; rather a prisoner would have been taken by police car to the gates of the institution and handed over with a 'Warrant for Committal', authorising the prison authorities to accept the young offender. And so on that Friday afternoon, Lorcan Bale's life as a teenager ended and his life as a prison inmate began, at the moment when the assistant chief officer confirmed that the warrant was in order. After stating his name and address, the boy was taken to a waiting area just inside the prison gates where he put his signature to a large A3 document, the prison register. Without delay, Bale was then escorted across a small courtyard that was overlooked by the house where the governor lived. Looking up, he would have seen twin chimney stacks, which to the casual eye appear to be of identical height, but which are in fact asymmetrical, one being marginally taller than the other. These funnels were an example of a low-tech but extremely effective air-conditioning system: under the right weather conditions, a steady sea breeze would blow cold air into one chimney stack, causing the other to expel warm foul air trapped within the prison interior. On a good day, cool, fresh air could fully circulate throughout the building in only five minutes.

St Patrick's Institution, opened in 1856, is architecturally based upon the design of London's Pentonville Prison. When constructed, the basement area was built with concave arches, meaning that the more weight added by the creation of additional floors above, the stronger the foundations became. The décor and furnishings were chosen for functionality, not aesthetics, giving the place a bare, spartan look. The walls were two-tone cream, the floors were wood covered in places by thick green linoleum, and throughout the prison there could be found creaking barred doors secured by heavy-duty brass locks. While the interior has been somewhat modernised over recent years, the exterior grey stone façade with tiny windows has barely changed. If a young horse thief from the 1800s were to step into a time machine and see it as it is today, he would likely notice very few differences.

On the other side of the courtyard and through a sloping corridor, the teenager walked down 17 stone steps holding the black handrail until he had reached the basement level. At the bottom of the steps, he turned right and passed through a narrow door that led directly to the shower block, a three-sided room with whitewashed walls where newly arrived inmates washed in tepid water. There he undressed. The civilian clothes he had entered wearing would be bagged up and put away until the day of his release, each item carefully logged in the clothing register. While today's juvenile prisoners record hoodies, tracksuits and trainers, the 1973 register had spaces for garments that fashion has long forgotten including drawers, collars and braces. A prisoner would also have to declare any pawn tickets he may have possessed, as these were considered currency. Records of physical appearance were also kept– scars and tattoos were the most obvious, but also the prisoner's height, eye colour, hair colour and any missing teeth. Lorcan Maolmuire Bale's height was recorded as 5 ft 6 in. Finally with the legalities, formalities and practicalities out of the way, a warder handed Bale the standard issue 'arrivals kit': a comb, two small cream soaps with the word 'Welcome' imprinted in italics on each bar, a toothbrush, toothpaste, a facecloth and shampoo, a hand towel, bath towel, two sheets and a pillow case. His remaining bed kit – a blanket and a pillow – would await him in his cell.

After taking a shower, the boy was issued with the remand prisoner's uniform, different from that worn by convicted prisoners, but still a distinct step down from his previous outlandish and extravagant style. The teenager would now have to put behind him his days of wearing purple flares, cheesecloth shirts and Huck Finn straw hats. From now on clothes were not an expression of individuality but a uniform of conformity. Each morning's outfit would be the same: a green shirt, a grey corduroy jacket, grey cord slacks and a V-necked grey jumper.

Following photographing and fingerprinting, the teenager was escorted up the stairs to 'the circle', a large octahedral area that formed the centrepiece of the prison. In a design also borrowed from Pentonville Prison, an officer – this duty would fall to a 'chief officer class two', known as a 'two bar' due to his shoulder strips – had a view of the whole prison from the circle, and so could be an all-seeing presence in the closed world that surrounded him. Radiating from the circle were three wings, designated as B, C and D (A wing had been decommissioned years earlier). Within each wing were three levels – for instance, B wing would have B1, B2 and B3 – each with individual cell blocks running on either side of the long corridors. B wing tended to accommodate offenders between the ages of 16 and 18; prisoners from rural Ireland, 'the country boys', would find themselves in C wing; D wing was home to young Dublin prisoners. Within these broad parameters, Lorcan Bale was now ready to be 'classed'. The class officer was brusque and businesslike with the new arrival, not because of his nature but because he was bound by strict regulations. The Rules for the Government of Prisons, 1947, strictly prohibited any form of fraternisation, including friendly banter, between officers and prisoners:

> Rule 114. (1) An officer shall not allow any familiarity on the part of a prisoner towards himself or any other officer or servant of the prison; nor shall he on any account speak of his duties, or of any matters of discipline or prison arrangement, within the hearing of a prisoner.
>
> (2) An officer shall not speak to a prisoner unnecessarily, nor shall he, by word, gesture, or demeanour, do anything which may tend to irritate any prisoner.

'Lorcan Bale – D1, half way down on the right-hand side,' was the class officer's decision. The boy nodded and made his way to the landing where his cell door was open. Like all young offenders in St Patrick's Institution, his was a single cell. This was in no way a punishment: he was not in solitary confinement as such; there would be many opportunities to leave the confines of the cell during the day and mix with other inmates. It was simply due to the prisoner's young age, a boy who at just 16 was still a juvenile in the eyes of the law and therefore judged to need a degree of insulation from adult prisoners. Additionally, as a remand prisoner, he would not normally be allowed to mingle with sentenced prisoners, though this rule was not always strictly enforced.

The door to his cell was open. If the new arrival had stood outside to survey the cell, there would not have been much to see. It was 13 feet long by 7 feet wide with most of the floor space being taken up by a single bed, a free-standing steel dormitory-style army billet. Beside it sat a bedside table, while on the opposite side of the room was a small writing desk with a matching chair.

Unlike today's cells, there was no toilet; prisoners were issued with a pail, a metal bucket that was emptied each morning in a practice known as 'slopping out'. Opposite the door was a window with 14 panes of glass. It was relatively wide given the tiny area of the cell, measuring 4 feet by 18 inches. The cell was far from luxurious, or even comfortable. Should the teenager feel the need to contact a warder after lockdown, he could pull a handle which triggered a string release system connected to a panel on the landing. A tiny window would open up revealing the cell number of the prisoner seeking attention. It was a low-tech, yet fit for purpose, one-way call bell system.

That evening Bale received his first prison meal, the standard issue for all new arrivals: sliced pan bread and butter, a half pint of milk (served in a Tetra Pak carton, glass bottles being prohibited) and a jug of tea. Contemporaries have no memories of any particular incident surrounding Lorcan Bale's arrival, so one can assume that he settled down quietly for the night, lost in his own thoughts, replaying the events of the previous day and perhaps only now realising just how they were going to affect him in the years ahead.

The next morning at 9.10 a.m., Lorcan Bale stood on parade before the governor of St Patrick's Institution along with the other remand prisoners of his age. For the new arrival, one who was likely to be within these walls for many years to come, Governor Donoghue outlined the main rules of the prison. The full list would have taken over an hour to recount but for now the teenager was reminded of his position and the parameters associated with being a remand 'innocent until proven guilty' prisoner. Given his legal status and young age, the policy was to leave cell doors open between 7 a.m. and 7.30 p.m. in an effort to make the regime feel less oppressive. The sixteen year old was informed that he was required to take two periods of exercise each week, he would have one hour of schooling each day and that he could select books to read from the library, subject to them first being screened for suitability by the prison chaplain.

Governor Donoghue had a reputation for being tough but fair, a man who stuck rigidly to the prison rules. At governor's parade that Saturday morning, Lorcan Bale and the other inmates were reminded of the consequences of stepping out of line. A glance through the rulebook leaves little room for doubt:

Rule 68. A prisoner shall be guilty of a breach of prison discipline if he –

(1) Disobeys any order of the Governor or of any other officer or any prison regulation.

(2) Treats with disrespect any officer or servant of the prison or any visitor, or any person employed in connection with the prison.

(3) Is idle, careless, or negligent at work, or refuses to work.

(4) Is absent without leave from divine service, or prayers, or school instruction.

(5) Behaves irreverently at divine service or prayers.

(6) Swears, curses, or uses any abusive, insolent, threatening, or other improper language.

(7) Is indecent in language, act, or gesture.

(8) Commits a common assault upon another prisoner or any other person.

(9) Converses or holds intercourse with another prisoner without authority.

(10) Sings, whistles, or makes any unnecessary noise, or gives any unnecessary trouble.

(11) Leaves his cell or other appointed location, or his place of work, without permission.

(12) In any way disfigures or damages any part of the prison, or any article to which he may have access.

(13) Commits any nuisance.

(14) Has in his cell or possession any unauthorised article, or attempts to obtain such article.

(15) Gives to or receives from any person any unauthorised article whatever.

(16) In any other way offends against good order and discipline.

In those early days on remand, Lorcan Bale held regular meetings with his solicitor who would have kept him updated with the progress of his regular court appearances. As the notoriety of the murder spread among the law enforcement community, a number of Garda police drivers escorting the young prisoner to remand hearings would attempt to engage Bale in casual conversation, seeking some insight into the mind of the young killer. However the accused was well briefed, replying politely that his solicitor had advised him not to comment at this time. The court appearances themselves were procedural remand hearings, the first in Howth Court three days after his arrival in St Patrick's Institution. There District Justice O'Hagan ordered that he be returned to custody to appear again at Lucan court a fortnight later. That brief session resulted in another two week remand and so the cycle of court appearances and returns to custody continued, until a trial date was set for November, five months after the murder was committed.

Lorcan Bale also underwent psychiatric counselling to assess his state of mind and ability to stand trial. This important question – which is examined in some detail later in this book – was answered over the following months, when the professionals agreed after a number of sessions that Bale was not mentally ill and was in a fit state to face a murder trial.

Irish people are without doubt among the most eloquent in the world, a national trait that has produced many generations of fine orators, poets, musicians and writers. The downside of this love of the spoken word is that Ireland is also a country where it is virtually impossible to keep a secret. So it was that around this time news of a 'satanic child murderer' spread to the United States, where a New York priest with an interest in the occult heard of the teenager being held in a young offenders' remand prison in Dublin. The priest, a larger-than-life character with a broad South Bronx, Italian-American accent, boarded a flight to

Dublin and immediately began loudly pestering the authorities for a meeting with Lorcan Bale. His request was politely declined by police handling the case, but the cleric, having come so far, interpreted this refusal as a mere temporary setback. Redoubling his efforts, he somehow persuaded a young prison officer to let him into St Patrick's Institution late one night when most of the guards were off duty. At around midnight the priest was slipped through the gates and escorted to D wing, the temporary home of the young remand prisoner. Very quietly the prison officer slid back the spy hole built into the wooden door at eye level, and the priest pressed his cheek against the door. Without warning the cleric's legs buckled and he collapsed with a thud onto the floor. Moments later he came to and, ashen faced, announced, 'I have seen the face of evil.' He left St Patrick's hurriedly, made no more requests to see the young prisoner and returned without delay to New York.

Among juvenile prisoners awaiting trial, there was an established two-tier system under which repeat offenders were kept separate from new inmates. It was a very deliberate policy because the authorities believed that keeping the 'good eggs' separate from the 'bad' would prevent the good ones acquiring the infection of habitual criminality. Prison officers were under orders to strictly adhere to the policy:

> Rule 214. (1) All prisoners under the age of 17 who are on remand or awaiting trial, in these rules referred to as unconvicted juvenile prisoners, shall be formed into two divisions, being classed by the Governor and chaplain : –
> (a) Those who have not been in prison before and who are well-conducted in prison, who shall be kept separate from
> (b) Those who have been in prison before, or who misbehave in prison.

Despite the gravity of the crime of which he was accused, Lorcan Bale was placed in the 'good egg' category, based on the fact that he had no previous criminal record. In the future he would discover that his position as a middle class boy from a reputable family helped him gain certain privileges not generally offered to inmates from more deprived backgrounds.

He had other factors in his favour, including that his home life and experience at Coláiste Mhuire had made him familiar with the concept of having a daily routine. It would not be an exaggeration to say that many of the teenagers at St Patrick's were unaware that the meal of lunch was typically taken around 1 p.m., that Monday to Friday constituted the days of the working week, and that classes in school followed a rigid weekly timetable. While monotonous, the daily routine of the prison brought to some inmates a structure and stability they had never previously experienced. At 8 a.m. the cell doors would be unlocked and prisoners would slop out, wash, collect breakfast and return to their cells. At 9.15 a.m. prisoners would make their beds, tidy their cells and go to the library, the school or if they had a job in the prison, their place of work. Lunch would be collected at 12.15 p.m. and eaten in the cell. Between 2 p.m. and 4.15 p.m. there was more activity time, followed by tea and recreation, usually watching television. At 7.20 p.m. the young offenders would be required to collect a light supper and return to their cells. Lights out was at midnight, Monday to Sunday, it never varied.

This routine, while it did bring order and structure to the wings, must also have been interminably dull for many of the inmates. However, very occasionally an incident occurred that would become a talking point to counter the boredom, and on the last day of October 1973, while awaiting his murder trial, Lorcan Bale had a ringside seat to one of the most audacious prison escapes in twentieth century penal history. At some stage every prisoner thinks of escape, yet few attempt it and fewer still succeed. During his time in prison, Lorcan Bale made no escape attempts, though he was aware of a number of breakouts both from St Patrick's and from the adult prison next door, Mountjoy.

*

Mountjoy Prison was in the same complex as St Patrick's, separated from it by a high wall. The adult and juvenile prisons were managed as distinct entities: they shared a geographic location, but each had its own governors, wardens and staff. Some of the country's most notorious prisoners were held in Mountjoy, including a number of Irish Republican Army (IRA) leaders involved in the Northern Ireland conflict, whose violence had escalated significantly over the previous four years. The young inmates at St Patrick's would have been aware of the presence of Mountjoy next door, indeed some of their number would someday find themselves serving time there.

The conflict in Northern Ireland was deepening; 1973 was a year in which IRA and loyalist paramilitary violence escalated, and both the British and Irish governments were resorting to increasingly draconian methods in an attempt to keep a lid on paramilitary activity. South of the border, in the Irish Republic, the Fine Gael party had entered government promising no sanctuary for those who sought goals that might undermine the state. Because few witnesses were willing to give evidence against IRA members, a new law – The Offences against the State Act – was introduced under which an IRA suspect could be formally accused of being a member of an illegal organisation, with no requirement to present evidence, but purely on the opinion of a superintendent in the *Garda Síochána*, the Irish police force. It was internment in all but name. IRA suspects went before a judge sitting without a jury at Dublin's Special Criminal Court; the accused would refuse to recognise the court, no defence would be offered, and a sentence of at least a year in Mountjoy would be handed down.

In September 1973 Seamus Twomey, the chief of staff of the IRA (its most senior leader) faced the Special Criminal Court on a charge of membership of the IRA. Predictably, when asked to plead, he sneered contempt for the proceedings entirely, declaring, 'I refuse to recognise this British-orientated quisling court.' His statement did nothing to sway the judge who found him guilty and jailed him for five years. This left the IRA's leadership severely undermined, with Twomey and two other senior republicans, J.B. O'Hagan and Kevin Mallon, all incarcerated in Mountjoy Prison.

With three of its most senior activists incarcerated, the IRA planned a jailbreak to free Twomey, O'Hagan and Mallon and return them to the ranks. Within weeks a plan had been put together: some commercial explosives would be smuggled into Mountjoy. Then the gelignite would be used to blow a hole in a door leading to the exercise yard, where, on the far side, a rope ladder would be waiting, slung across the wall by local sympathisers. The trio would scale the wall and be met by a waiting getaway car. But to the great disappointment of the IRA gang, prison guards spotted the rope ladder before the escape began. The plan failed. It was time to consider something more drastic.

The Provisional IRA (Provo) leadership then gave the green light to a bold and ambitious scheme to extricate Twomey, O'Hagan and Mallon, not on foot, but by air. This was not an original idea. Some months earlier, the same leadership had been considering using a helicopter to pluck Republican activist Gerry Adams, then interned without trial, from Her Majesty's Prison Maze – also known as Long Kesh – outside Belfast. The idea was then rejected because the British army had armoured helicopters stationed nearby. Mountjoy, however, had no such military might in its shadow. All the Provos needed to free three of their top brass was a foolproof plan, a helicopter and someone to fly it. Sometime during October of that year, the offices of Irish Helicopters, near Dublin airport, were approached by a Mr Leonard, a sharply dressed man with a mid-Atlantic drawl, who described himself as an American photographer. He told them he was planning an aerial shoot in County Laois, some 60 miles from Dublin. The manager showed Mr Leonard a five-seater Alouette II, a popular machine that was in use worldwide. The 'American photographer' said the craft was perfect and booked it for Wednesday, 31 October.

The weather was good, offering ideal flying conditions when Mr Leonard arrived at Irish Helicopters to meet his pilot for this assignment, Captain Thompson Boyes. They took off and the pilot was directed to fly west and set down in a field in Stradbally, County Laois, where he was told they would collect Mr Leonard's photographic gear. However just moments after they touched down, two armed and masked men raced from the undergrowth and hijacked the Alouette. The gang told Captain Boyes that he would not be harmed so long as he followed their instructions to the letter. Mr Leonard left the scene accompanied by one of the gunmen, while the other, armed with a pistol and an Armalite rifle, took a seat in the helicopter. Captain Boyes was instructed to fly towards Dublin without alerting air traffic control, and when there to follow the Royal Canal, which skirts Mountjoy Prison. Approaching the capital, the hijacker revealed to the pilot that their mission was to land in the exercise courtyard of Mountjoy and to pick up three passengers with a minimum of delay.

That afternoon Lorcan Bale was quietly lost in the routine of working in the workshop, reading and exercise, when a commotion was heard outside. Shortly after 3.30 p.m., as Mountjoy prisoners were playing a football game, an unfamiliar sound added to the cacophony of the courtyard: that of the gas turbine of a French-made single engine helicopter booming over the prison walls. So unusual was the spectacle that a prison officer on duty initially assumed that they were about to receive a surprise visit from Irish Defence Minister Paddy Donegan. However it did not take long to realise this was far from the case. This prison officer and the seven other guards on duty were quickly surrounded by prisoners – fists flew as it became obvious that a daring escape attempt was in progress. Within seconds of the helicopter touching down, the three passengers had boarded: Twomey, Mallon and O'Hagan. In the chaos that followed, one officer is reported to have shouted, 'Close the gates, close the fucking gates!' A few minutes later Captain Thompson Boyes' ordeal ended, when he touched down at Baldoyle racecourse a few miles north of Mountjoy. He was not harmed, as promised by his hijackers, and his passengers even bade him farewell as they sped off to freedom in a waiting stolen taxi.

The escape was front-page news across the globe and proved to be a huge embarrassment to the Irish government, especially in the light of their election on a 'law and order' platform. Nobody was surprised to see the IRA reaping massive propaganda value from the successful escape. While police forces across Europe hunted for the Mountjoy three, the German current affairs magazine *Der Spiegel* secured an exclusive interview with Seamus Twomey, who was more than happy to furnish German readers with the finer detail of what was termed 'the escape of the century'.

Irish rebel band, The Wolfe Tones, weighed in with a ballad commemorating the events at Mountjoy. It was immediately banned by the Irish government, which of course only served to guarantee its popularity: 'The Helicopter Song' sold 12,000 copies the first week of its release and shot to number one in the Irish charts.

Up like a bird and high over the city
'Three men are missing,' I heard the warder cry
'Sure it must have been a bird that flew into the prison
Or one of those new Ministers,' said the warder from
    Mountjoy.

Early one evening as the branchmen they were sleeping
A little helicopter flew in from the sky
Down into the yard where some prisoners were
    walking
'Get ready for inspection,' said the warder in the Joy.

Down in the yard through the pushing and the shoving
Three of the prisoners they climbed upon the bird
And up and away they went into the grey skies
'I think someone escaped,' said the warder in the Joy.

Over in the Dáil they were drinking gin and brandy
The minister for justice was soaking up the sun
Then came this little message that some prisoners
    were escaping
'I think it's three of the Provos,' said the warder in the
    Joy.

'Search every hole search every nook and cranny
Let no man rest until these men are found
For this cannot happen to a law-and-order government'
'I think you'll never find them,' said the warder in
    Mountjoy.

Eventually the Mountjoy Three were tracked down and arrested again, but by then the damage had well and truly been done. Mallon was recaptured dancing in a hotel six weeks after the breakout, O'Hagan was caught in Dublin after fourteen months on the run, while the IRA's Chief of Staff, Seamus Twomey, enjoyed over four years of freedom until he was finally re-arrested after a high street car chase ended, quite ironically, not far from Mountjoy.

Many in St Patrick's Institution considered the events at the adult prison next door to be something of a circus – a welcome diversion from the drudgery of the daily routine. Lorcan Bale, however, had another focus: his trial.

Bale's trial had drawn interest from many newspapers and international press agencies, within Ireland and also from the UK, the United States and Canada. For weeks the police press office in Dublin had been bombarded with enquiries about the case but because a trial was imminent, and could be prejudiced by reporting, they were severely limited in what they could say. The absence of facts prompted the growth of rumours, which in turn fuelled even greater interest. The case had all the elements of a media sensation: the terrible murder of an innocent child, the assailant also being a juvenile, and, most salacious of all, the satanic overtones of the murder. Few if any reporters knew the case in accurate detail, but among their company the use of the word 'crucified' was enough to guarantee that they were eagerly anticipating a ringside seat at what would undoubtedly be the trial of the year. So on 27 November 1973, in a packed courtroom at Dublin's Central Criminal Court, Lorcan Maolmuire Bale faced a charge of the murder of seven-year-old John Horgan. In charge of proceedings was a highly respected judge, Mr Justice Kenny. Representing the prosecution was Mr Gerard Clarke, Senior Counsel for the Attorney General, while the defence barrister was one of Ireland's most colourful legal figures, Seamus Sorahan. Senior Counsel Sorahan was a criminal barrister, popular among his peers and renowned for his flamboyant use of language. A compulsive book collector, he owned dozens of weighty volumes, notably books about great trials – including the Nuremberg trials at the end of World War Two – and tomes about peripheral aspects of the law.

After the jury was sworn in, the case began with the accused being asked to respond to the charge in the form of a plea: guilty or not guilty. The 16 year old rose, faced Mr Justice Kenny and uttered just one word: 'Guilty.' This plea meant that the jury's services were no longer needed and so they were discharged. It also had a secondary effect; it meant that there was no need to present evidence to the jury, a long and time-consuming part of any trial. The plea meant Bale's trial would be completed that same day. There is very little that defence barrister Seamus Sorahan could have done on behalf of his young client. The guilty verdict was inevitable given the overwhelming evidence against him; the trial was more a formality to pass the necessary sentence. There was an opportunity for the defence barrister to put on record material facts on mitigation, and the matter that the accused had no previous criminal record, so that these facts would be available to the Minister of Justice when deciding years later when the right time would be to release the prisoner on license.

Both Mr Justice Kenny and defence barrister Seamus Sorahan praised the work of psychiatrist Dr Brian McCaffrey and psychologist Maureen Gaffney for the reports made on Lorcan Bale while he was in custody. Prosecuting barrister Gerard Clarke stated that inquiries into the murder were led by Garda Detective Inspector Reynolds and eventually a full statement was made by the accused as all the facts became clear. For the journalists in the press gallery, particularly those who had crossed the Atlantic to report to their readers the ebb and flow of what they expected to be a sensational satanic murder trial, this was the worst possible result. With an immediate guilty plea from a juvenile and no evidence read into open court, they were left with just enough reportable facts to merit a couple of paragraphs on the inside pages, the barest of stories which was sure to be glossed over by most readers.

Following the guilty plea, Justice Kenny's primary role was to pass sentence and to send the teenage murderer to the only appropriate place of detention in the state, St Patrick's Institution, where he had been on remand for the previous five months. The order that remains on file among the dusty records of the Central Criminal Court is short and to the point:

> Recommend that the convicted person Lorcan Maolmuire Bale be detained in St Patrick's Institution until he is 21 and then transferred to another prison. Recommend that Dr Brian McCaffrey and Miss Maureen Gaffney Clinical Psychologist in consultation with Dr McGrath be allowed to visit him while serving his sentence.
>
> Lorcan Maolmuire Bale to be kept in penal servitude for life.

Returning in a black prison van to St Patrick's that Tuesday afternoon, we have no way of knowing what was running through the boy's mind. Those four words, 'penal servitude for life', must surely have been foremost in his thoughts. He must have wondered how long he would be expected to serve. Today the typical life sentence prisoner in Ireland serves on average seventeen-and-a-half years. A few high-profile lifers have served considerably longer sentences, including Malcolm McArthur, who in 1982 bludgeoned to death a nurse who was sunbathing in Dublin's Phoenix Park. McArthur pleaded guilty to the murder charge in a trial that was completed in just five minutes. At the time of writing, McArthur was being considered for parole, almost 30 years after the crime. But on that cool November day in 1973, Lorcan Bale could have hoped for a shorter than average sentence; after all he was only 16 when the offence took place and, if properly rehabilitated, so the wisdom ran, might have a decent chance of a productive life in the world outside. But on the other hand he had to consider the gravity of the offence. This was not just any murder, but the murder of a child, committed by a child. The prisoner was in new territory – he had committed a grave crime, the gravest of all, and society demanded that he must atone. He could be certain that St Patrick's would be his home until his 21st birthday, in four-and-a-half years' time, after which, according to Mr Justice Kenny, he would be transferred to an adult prison. With good behaviour, he must have been reasonably confident of release before the age of 30, but much could happen in the intervening years.

Inside the prison walls, his status immediately changed that afternoon. As a convicted sentenced prisoner, Bale was issued with different clothes to distinguish him from remand prisoners. Where previously his visible status was 'innocent until proven guilty', a citizen still with a chance of unblemished release, now he was convicted, and his status demanded that watchers know it on sight. His new garb comprised a denim jacket, a shirt and denim jeans – known affectionately as 'cardboard' due to their extreme stiffness. The shoes were quite different to the trainers worn by today's prisoners; '70s inmates wore mottled leather boots, nicknamed 'crocks' due to their similarity to crocodile hide.

His young age gave Bale certain privileges not afforded to adult prisoners. As a convicted juvenile, there was an effort made to ease the harshness of the system. He was allowed special library books as well as books of general academic instruction; juvenile offenders were given jobs in workshops, or in the outdoors – usually doing gardening; in due course he would be instructed in a trade, which could be useful to him on release; and in recognition of the need for physical development, he would be expected to take part in a daily physical drill in addition to regular walks around the compound.

And as well as being a convicted juvenile, Bale had also become a 'penal servitude prisoner'. Penal servitude prisoners were those on life sentences. They were treated differently by other inmates and warders alike. One would expect that a murderer sentenced to a lifetime of penal servitude would be placed in the harshest of prison conditions, yet in many ways the opposite was true. Penal servitude prisoners were not merely waiting in prison to serve out their sentence, they were in prison for *life*, or close to; many would die within prison walls. Perhaps the authorities thought it wise not to antagonise men who, in the end, were the most dangerous of all prisoners, because they had nothing to lose. There was an unwritten rule that penal servitude prisoners were outside the norm, that, because of the enormity of their sentence, they should be treated with distance and even a certain respect. Today this unwritten rule has been formalised with the establishment of a 'lifers' group that meets regularly with the prison authorities to discuss areas of common interest.

Lorcan Bale met many people in his years in prison, and a number of them have agreed to be interviewed for this book. Most did so on condition of anonymity, but common to all were memories of an inmate who was unlike any other. Lorcan Bale took a firm decision that he would become a model prisoner, though not a conventional one, that he would put his head down and do his time and perhaps, someday, be released. In those early months, fellow prisoners and warders remember him as a pale, quiet youth who spoke little and did not make friends with any other convicts. During the day, he spent most of his working hours upstairs in the tailor's shop with warder Gerry Chapman, making and repairing trousers. His own 'cardboards' were perfectly pressed, his shirt crease-free and his hair always neatly combed. Around this time, the sallow skinned teenager spent hours scrubbing the wooden floorboards of his cell until they were ash white. This was not unusual, some prisoners were known to varnish their cell floors as protection from splinters, but according to a prison officer who patrolled the wings at this time, Lorcan Bale had a more unusual reason for his fastidiousness.

The officer explained:

> Using paint that he had got hold of in art study, Lorcan painted a black pentagram on the floor of his cell, and then with five straight brush strokes painted an identical matching five-pointed star on the ceiling. This wasn't some bit of rough graffiti – this was art, perfectly painted in perfect symmetry.

I asked why Bale had been permitted to have this symbol in his cell, something that would never be countenanced today. The officer hesitated before saying, 'I'm really not sure. Perhaps it was easier to allow him to paint the pentagrams than to create an incident by making him remove it.' The pentagram as a religious symbol has a place in the history of many faiths including Islam and Christianity, however most modern Christians now reject the symbol, viewing its adoption by various pagan groups as a sign of its links to satanism. Indeed the nineteenth-century French writer Eliphas Levi believed that how the symbol was positioned determined its message.

> A reversed pentagram, with two points projecting upwards, is a symbol of evil and attracts sinister forces because it overturns the proper order of things and demonstrates the triumph of

matter over spirit. It is the goat of lust attacking the heavens with its horns, a sign execrated by initiates.

The flaming star, which, when turned upside down, is the hieroglyphic sign of the goat of black magic, whose head may be drawn in the star, the two horns at the top, the ears to the right and left, the beard at the bottom. It is the sign of antagonism and fatality. It is the goat of lust attacking the heavens with its horns. Let us keep the figure of the Five-pointed Star always upright, with the topmost triangle pointing to heaven, for it is the seat of wisdom, and if the figure is reversed, perversion and evil will be the result.

Less highbrow LaVeyan satanists – and we know that Bale had a copy of Anton LaVey's book *The Satanic Bible* – use the pentagram as a sign of religious rebellion, the three downward points symbolising rejection of the Christian holy Trinity.

Aside from the double pentagrams, the boy's cell was quite dark after he had hung heavy curtains across the bars. He had no interest in going 'on the window', a practice during lockdown of prisoners communicating with each other by shouting out of their windows at full volume. Where other prisoners had posters of topless page-three girls taped to their walls, Bale's cell was decorated with pictures of nuns and angels. How he was allowed to get away with painting the pentagrams is beyond the comprehension of those involved in present-day prison management. Today, such conduct would simply not be permitted. What makes it even more difficult to understand is that his actions appear to be a flagrant breach of the prison's clear policy on the spiritual welfare of inmates.

Rule 52. No books or printed papers intended for the religious instruction of prisoners shall be admitted but those chosen by the chaplain of the persuasion to which the prisoner belongs; provided that, in case there may be a difference of opinion between the chaplain and the minister with respect to books or papers proposed to be admitted for the religious

> instruction of a prisoner, reference shall be made to his bishop
> or constituted ecclesiastical authority, whose decision shall be
> final; and, subject to such permission of the minister as
> aforesaid, all books or printed papers admitted into any prison
> for the religious instruction of prisoners belonging to any
> other persuasion, and who are visited by a clergyman of such
> persuasion, shall be approved by such clergyman.

Prison chaplains were enormously influential at the time; aside from supervising the young inmates' spiritual welfare, they remain a useful set of eyes on the lookout for prisoners showing the early telltale signs of depression. Today St Patrick's Institution has two chaplains who by all accounts carry out fine work. In the '70s there was one Catholic priest ministering to all the young inmates. In Ireland the vast majority of the prison population would have been Catholic; for the very rare prisoner who may have been attached to another faith such as the Anglican Church of Ireland, then an alternative clergyman could be found. On committal, each prisoner must declare their religion, a question which might well have presented Lorcan Bale with some difficulty. While he was of course baptised into the Roman Catholic faith, the rather extreme anti-Christian nature of his crime would have made ticking the 'Catholic' box inaccurate, somewhat ironic, and offensive to other practicing Catholics. He would hardly have declared himself as a satanist to the prison reception officer but, if accepted, such a declaration might have exempted him from religious instruction and attendance. Lorcan Bale's prison papers are not a matter of public record, his ink mark on the committal register is under lock and key, archived in the Irish Ministry of Justice. So we have no way of determining his perceived religious affiliation, though it is most likely that he would have been entered as being a member of the Roman Catholic church. After all, he was initiated into the Church, and this was the denomination of 99 percent of the prison population.

Assuming that he did attend Sunday Mass, Bale would have been present in the most aesthetically pleasing part of St Patrick's, also the brightest section of the prison. The chapel is an impressive modern style church, which seats around 120 prisoners. Lit from both sides by six large, Georgian-style sash windows, each with twelve panes, the architecture and glass combine to create an impression of a holy space filled with natural light.

Church would have been a weekly distraction from the routine of prison life. For most prisoners, the primary challenge of every day was to deal with the perpetual boredom of hours confined to a cell, the loneliness and the isolation. It took quite an effort to avoid falling prey to melancholy thoughts, in those darkest moments of introspection that too much time affords. Situated directly above the church, the prison library was an oasis that brought sanctuary to many, including Bale. Books were one of the only ways that the outside world entered the prison. Next to the library was the laundry, a tough, hot working environment where prison warders would supervise their young charges doing the hard physical work of washing, scrubbing, rinsing and hanging denim prison-wear on steaming 30-foot-long heater rails. It was backbreaking work, all undertaken by hand. While no prison jobs were easy, neither could it have been seen as slave labour. In return for their efforts, prisoners received a gratuity, or 'grat', a tiny amount of symbolic paper money, which could be exchanged for cigarettes, sweets, lemonade or cards. Cigarettes were a popular currency, and in those days just about every prisoner smoked in their cells, in the recreation hall – anywhere really, as smoking restrictions were minimal in Ireland at that time. Unlike today, though smoking was universal, the use of drugs was rare; there simply was no great culture of drug use, beyond the expected tobacco, alcohol and small amounts of cannabis resin. The narcotic supply chains that today bring such substances to towns and cities – and prisons – with frightening efficiency had not yet been properly formed. That was to change in the '80s with the importation to Ireland by local criminal gangs of vast quantities of cheap heroin – a new vice, yet one that did not take long to find its way into the nation's jails. The sudden boom in the popularity of intravenous drugs came at the worst possible time, during the ascendancy of the AIDS/HIV epidemic. The dangers were less well-known, users tending not to be aware of the risks of sharing needles: the impact on the prison population was devastating. While less prevalent today thanks to structured addiction programmes, the misuse of drugs in jails remains an enormous concern for the prison authorities.

From his early days on remand, other inmates felt that Lorcan Bale was different, that he stood apart from them in some indefinable way. While they all wore the identical prison uniform, his demeanour, his languid pale physique, even his quiet nature made him stand out from the crowd. Ordinarily being different – and a convicted child killer – would have resulted in harassment and torment for him, but Bale, more by accident than design, managed to avoid the very worst horrors of prison life. Rumours began to spread that this teenager had strange powers, that he was in St Patrick's for being responsible for the crucifixion of a young child, that when he was free he used to conduct strange black mass ceremonies in his attic, that he worshipped the devil chanting in a foreign language while seated on the odd black star on the floor of his cell with a black cat curled up outside his cell door. A prison officer stationed in St Patrick's spoke about an 'eerie evil odour' that emanated from the teenager's cell, though the same officer also described the boy as being deep and quite intelligent.

Others had praise for the teenager and spoke about the range of his creative powers; certainly he was a gifted artist whose work showed extraordinary detail and inexplicable depth. A few also made the claim that he could write backwards in mirrored writing. In prison he further developed his musical interest. Before the murder, he had practiced the violin intensely, becoming one of the finest young players of his age in the country. In prison Bale taught himself to play the banjo under the supervision of a prison officer from Galway, Mick Mulvany, who, like his young prisoner, was a talented musician and a fluent Irish speaker. Prisoners in the cells on either side of his would complain that they could not sleep due to Bale's continuous chanting. They wondered when he managed to sleep, or if he even slept at all.

As a cult of Lorcan Bale gradually emerged, separating the myth from the reality was not always easy. Today fellow prisoners who were behind bars at the same time recall the common view was that here was a fairly likeable young man, yet one from whom it was best to keep your distance. While the young convict did nothing to encourage the aura that was developing around him, neither did he discourage it. Naturally he ate the same food as the other prisoners and got to know a few of them reasonably well. He also showed a certain degree of compassion, particularly towards those raised in a less privileged background than his own. Occasionally there would be a shortage of teachers in the school wing and Bale would agree to take a class, often providing one-to-one instruction for juvenile inmates with reading difficulties. When not immersed in a book, he would settle down to watch television in the recreation hall, following a strict routine of always sitting in the same chair in the front row of the hall. It was in this room, which looked no different to a typical hospital waiting room, that an incident occurred in which Bale was entirely blameless, yet that elevated the cult of Lorcan Bale to near-mythical status.

In the second year of Bale's sentence, St Patrick's welcomed a new arrival. In truth, John McCarthy would be better described as part of the borstal's furniture, having already served time for a range of petty crimes. John was a traveller, a people who are increasingly accepted today as an indigenous Irish ethnic group, but in the '70s were the subject of widespread dislike and contempt. Travellers would set up camp on the edge of town and made their living from buying and selling – horse dealing and the like. Many were illiterate, most were poorly educated; alcoholism and low-level criminality were rife in their community. In many respects they found themselves at the bottom rung of society, at the end of the pecking order when it came to employment, housing and healthcare.

John McCarthy's path to St Patrick's Institution and eventual contact with Lorcan Bale began in his home town of Limerick on a Saturday night in March 1975. In an act of stupidity that seemed to have no reason other than, perhaps, bored teenagers seeking kicks, 18-year-old John and his friend stole a car and raced it crazily through the Patrickswell district of the town. Unsurprisingly, they soon crashed, hitting another car parked by the roadside. Both young men were injured, but not severely, and they quickly fled the scene on foot, their hands and faces covered with blood. Minutes later they were spotted walking along the roadside by a passing police patrol car, and were immediately arrested. Neither boy would come quietly; Stephen Cawley ran off while John McCarthy struck Garda Patrick Fox with a firm right hook, landing square on the officer's mouth. The assailant was overpowered and bundled into the back of the patrol car, where he berated his captors with a tirade of foul and abusive language, an outpouring that continued unabated until he found himself locked up in a police cell for the night. Stealing a car was seen as a moderately serious offence, but punching an officer of the *Garda Síochána* was an upping of McCarthy's game for which he would be expected to atone. A week later at Limerick District Court, the youngster pleaded guilty to four charges: assault on a Garda, dangerous driving, driving without insurance, and using a motor-propelled vehicle without the consent of the owner. Given the severity of the charges, his sentence of three months' imprisonment in St Patrick's Institution was relatively light. However, despite his young age, John had a long criminal history and a week later would be back in court to face further charges relating to various other driving offences that occurred before the assault. Picking up an additional two month sentence, he was in court again six weeks later for receiving stolen property – a leather jacket. The judge sentenced him to another three months for the last felony. With concurrent sentencing, remission and good behaviour, McCarthy could be expected to serve in total some 14 weeks, and a release date of 8 July 1975 was set.

The classing system in St Patrick's for the most part separated the Dublin offenders from those raised in rural Ireland. John McCarthy was from Limerick and felt more comfortable with the country lads, and once settled in the institution did his best to avoid the Dubliners, including the child murderer Lorcan Bale. Shortly after his committal, McCarthy was sent to work with a group tasked with breaking up concrete blocks. This detail was under the supervision of Prison Officer Thomas Quinn, whose twin roles were to help in the maintenance of the prison and to oversee work details. This particular work group was made up of a combination of Dublin and country lads; the Limerick boy avoided the city crowd, indeed one day he asked Officer Quinn whether he could include some other Limerick boys in the party – a request that was granted. The supervising officer recalls that the new arrivals seemed to make the Limerick boy happier and that he settled into the work, rarely speaking unless spoken to. Officer Quinn recalled, 'I don't know whether he could write, but he had cowboy books so I assumed he could read. I didn't think he was very bright in the educational sense. But he was a placid lad, a good worker and one that I never had any occasion to reprimand.'

One of the Limerick boys who joined the work party at McCarthy's request was 16-year-old Eugene Glasheen; the pair had been friends since primary school. He revealed that John did not get on with his brother Michael, who was also an inmate at St Patrick's, and that any mention of his sibling risked triggering John's volatile temper. 'He usually got mad if any mention was made of his brother appearing at court, or if he was told that he was cheating at push penny,' revealed Eugene, adding, 'I think the fact that he got so many prison sentences depressed him a bit. Sometimes he was in a bad frame of mind or depressed but I didn't pay much attention to this as other inmates are the same from time to time.'

Another Limerick teenager on the detail was 19-year-old John

McNamara, serving a 12 month stretch in the jail, a friend of McCarthy's from previous terms in St Patrick's. McNamara considered himself to be McCarthy's best friend in the institution, even closer than his brother and fellow inmate Michael McCarthy. He too spoke about meeting in the recreation hall in the early evening where the pair would play push penny and rings. Both games of skill, push penny – also known as 'shove ha'penny' – is a pub game where players attempt to shove coins up a board so that they fall between horizontal lines at the top. At first glance it appears simple, but it requires a steady hand and a degree of luck, and with more losers than winners, an even temper is essential. Rings is a game that was popular at one time in Ireland's many pubs. Players would throw small rubber rings towards a shield-shaped board in an effort to hook the rings to the board. Not dissimilar to darts, success at rings required exceptional calmness and concentration, neither of which McCarthy had in great supply. On the contrary, he was agitated and quick tempered. The prison hospital orderly was concerned enough about McCarthy's welfare to bring him to the attention of Medical Officer Dr Kilgallen, who found the youth to be physically well and noted that 'conversation with him revealed a history of recidivism' – a repeated relapsing into criminal or delinquent behaviour. He added that the boy, while physically and mentally well, 'was semi-literate with a low frustration tolerance'.

Around that time tensions were higher than usual in the prison. There was talk of escape plans, though mostly this was just idle speculation and wishful thinking. A prisoner in Mountjoy adult prison across the wall had taken his own life by hanging, while in St Patrick's an inmate Kevin Kiernan set his own cell on fire. Mercifully for him, the fire was extinguished before he suffered the serious effects of smoke. Put together, these events are likely to have had an unsettling effect on some of the more vulnerable inmates.

Then on or around Tuesday, 13 May 1975, two months into John McCarthy's sentence and almost two years after Lorcan Bale was incarcerated, the two boys met one evening in the recreation hall. They couldn't have been more different characters: Bale was small, thin, quiet, educated, from a stable family, middle class, intelligent, a Dubliner, with no previous criminal record; McCarthy was a traveller, strong as an ox, working class, semi-literate, a Limerick lad with little regard for city types, with a long list of convictions despite his young age. Witnesses who were watching television or playing table tennis remember words being exchanged between the pair, though what the row was about has been long forgotten. What they do remember is that despite his small stature, Lorcan Bale stood up to John McCarthy, and though the argument never escalated to fists, it was loud and acrimonious. Disagreements and scuffles were commonplace in this environment, hardly surprising when dozens of adolescent boys are confined together, but subsequent events would push this particular day into a mythical legend in prison lore and further elevate the cult of Lorcan Bale.

The following day, Wednesday, 14 May, cell number 19, which was next to John McCarthy's cell, lay vacant, following the release of its occupant. McCarthy asked the prison authorities if his friend John McNamara could move to the empty cell so that he could share the company of a fellow Limerick teenager, a pal and a work colleague – indeed they were on the same concrete-block-breaking afternoon work detail. This request was granted and McNamara moved his belongings into cell D19.

Thursday, 15 May began like any other: doors unlocked, slopping out, breakfast, cell tidying, schooling, lunch. That afternoon at 3.30 p.m., while McCarthy was cutting blocks with McNamara and Bale was mending trousers in the tailor's workshop, a group of nine teenagers in the wood cutting yard caused a diversionary disturbance distracting the attention of the guards supervising their work detail. Moments later they were scaling the wall and they managed to reach the top just as the alarm sounded and pursuit began. Two of the boys panicked on hearing the siren and leapt onto the concrete below, an ill-advised action, which resulted in both of them breaking their legs. The remainder were more careful with their descent to freedom. Their liberty, however, was destined to be short-lived; by the time a search was mounted just minutes later, several of the group had plunged into the fetid, algal waters of the Royal Canal. This waterway had fallen into disrepair, having closed in 1953, but a group of conservation volunteers were at that time attempting to clear the detritus from the canal. They had not yet made great progress and it cannot have been pleasant for the aspiring escapees to swim through the filthy, numbingly cold water – only for their jailbreak to end when all but two were ignominiously hauled from the canal by the authorities. The remaining pair made it as far as Croke Park, Ireland's most famous football stadium, which stands almost a mile from the prison walls, before they too were apprehended and returned to St Patrick's Institution.

The escape attempt must surely have been on McCarthy and McNamara's minds when they met just before 6 p.m. that evening in the recreation hall. Over a few games of rings and push penny, they chatted about how they would spend their 'grat' money, which was due to be paid two days hence. McCarthy also speculated on whether it would be possible to fashion a small hole in the wall separating their cells so they could speak freely after lockdown. McCarthy was clearly lonely, confessing to his friend that since being committed to the prison two months earlier, he had received just one visitor, his girlfriend, Mary. After collecting their evening meals, the friends returned to their adjacent cells where the doors, as normal, were locked for the night at 8 p.m. While their conversation continued, it was anything but a quiet chat: going 'on the window' they were able to communicate but only by shouting loudly into the courtyard outside, McNamara recalling that McCarthy 'was in his usual good humour and appeared to be in good form'. After they finished talking, McNamara climbed into bed and began to read a book, when after about ten minutes he heard the bed in the next cell being moved. He thought nothing of it and drifted off to sleep.

An hour later 54-year-old prison officer George Fox clocked in to begin night duty. Normally this shift would have been uneventful, even tedious, with the prisoners locked in their cells and mostly asleep. With 26 years of exemplary service under his belt, Fox knew every nook and cranny of St Patrick's and was well regarded by warders and inmates alike. As usual, he began his rounds by walking the corridors of D wing, checking individually on each prisoner through the spy hole built into the wooden door. It was not long before he reached cell 17. Peering through the hole, the darkness slowly resolved into the outline of a figure hanging from the window. In the moment it took his eyes to adjust, his worst fears were confirmed: John McCarthy was hanging by a bed sheet tied around his neck, with his feet dangling just above the ground.

Without delay, Officer Fox ran to the end of the landing and shouted down to Assistant Chief Officer Peter Folan to come quickly and to bring the cell keys. Seconds later Folan unlocked the cell and bolted inside, along with four other officers. He and Fox cut the sheet with a penknife and laid the boy down on his bed before immediately applying artificial respiration. At this point, the Limerick teenager was still warm and the warders were sure that he could be revived if he received swift medical attention, so they ordered one of the junior officers to send for the hospital orderly Noel Edmonds, whose house was just outside the main gate. Ten minutes later, Edmonds ran into D wing and took over artificial respiration while they all waited for an ambulance to arrive. But despite the long minutes spent maintaining his vital functions, McCarthy was showing no signs of revival, so he was carried the short distance to the prison surgery where increasingly desperate attempts to restart his breathing were tried. Around 10 p.m. as an ambulance paramedic felt for the young man's pulse, it was clear that his short life had come to an end, confirmation, if any were needed, being provided by Dr Kilgallon on his arrival minutes later.

Later that evening the dead teenager's father was told the tragic news and the following day McCarthy's uncle, who had known the boy all of his life, arrived in the Dublin City Morgue where formal identification was made. A month later, at the Dublin Coroner's Court, the circumstances surrounding the death of John McCarthy were laid before a jury. The prison medical officer, Dr Kilgannon, testified, 'he may have been acting out of some impulse, but I would not think it was a deliberate suicide'. The governor of St Patrick's, Denis Donoghue, agreed, linking the death with an earlier suicide at Mountjoy prison. 'The publicity given to a recent hanging may have prompted him to some prank or experiment, which misfired with tragic consequences.' After hearing all of the evidence, the jury rejected the option of declaring the death of John McCarthy to be a suicide, and instead brought in the more sensitive verdict of accidental death.

So what had all this to do with Lorcan Bale? In truth, absolutely nothing. The facts and the testimony of those close to him pointed to John McCarthy being lonely and depressed, regretting the destructive path his life had taken. They suggest that in a moment of dark introspection he had accidentally taken his own life. However, in the confines of a prison, the lines between fact, fiction, speculation and rumour often blur, sometimes with unexpected consequences. The young inmates of St Patrick's knew that Lorcan Bale was different, an oddball who dabbled in the occult; they also knew that he was dangerous and that he had already taken an innocent life. Combining these factors with the very public argument between Bale and McCarthy days earlier in the recreation hall, it came to be believed that somehow Bale had cast a spell on the Limerick boy, a hex, which, through means unknown or forces unknowable, had resulted in his death. This was of course nonsense but despite the incredible nature of the rumour – or perhaps because of it – the idea grew wings, and was soon widely believed throughout the prison. Bale, it was said, had powers from 'the dark side'; and it would be unwise, perhaps even fatal, to cross him. As one inmate later said, 'From that day, nobody touched him.'

Fellow young offenders recall this time well. In prison lore a mythology grew up around Lorcan Bale simply because his audience – which included ill-educated and superstitious youngsters, many of whom were victims of appalling abuse at Ireland's industrial schools – simply had no clue how to react to him. His crime was no great secret, yet his method was so outrageous that he was in a way cocooned by that outrage. Once Bale was in this social mix, it was inevitable that boundaries would build up around him. Importantly, those closest to him at that time also state that he did not come into jail filled with remorse, yet the same people remember an extremely likeable teenager, not by nature an evil person, but one capable of great trespass, the ultimate trespass.

Despite Lorcan Bale being entitled to regular family visits, it was a year before Mr and Mrs Bale came to see their son in prison. It was said that they simply did not like coming to the jail, and disliked in particular the confined nature of a restrictive visit. A more likely explanation, however, is that the boy's parents found it difficult to come to terms with the enormity of his crime and with the knowledge that they – decent, upstanding, middle-class Irish Catholics, had raised a son who became a child killer. Of course they could not have known what their boy would grow up to do, but many parents, especially those who see themselves as having high moral standing, believe themselves at heart responsible for their children's actions, and feel that wickedness or evil on the part of their offspring has its roots in some deficiency of their own parenting. The Bale and the Horgan families had been more than good neighbours; they were close friends with the twin common bonds of firm religious faith and a belief in family values. The fact that Lorcan had so cruelly taken the life of the only child of these neighbours and friends must have made it doubly difficult for the Bales to look directly into the eyes of their son.

When they did eventually visit, they spoke only in Irish, the preferred language of the Bale family. Speaking Irish during a supervised prison visit was a right defined in *Bunreacht na hÉireann*, the Irish Constitution, the fundamental legal basis upon which all of the country's laws are drafted:

Article 8.
Section 1. The Irish language as the national language is the first official language.
Section 2. The English language is recognised as a second official language.

It was important that the prison officer who supervised the visit understood what was being said, so a solution was found in the person of a native Irish speaker from Galway, Officer Mick Mulvany, the banjo-playing prison warder, who, with occasional support from another fluent speaker, Officer Mick Ferris, would between them supervise all the family visits to Lorcan Bale.

There were other occasions when special efforts were made to accommodate the young prisoner. Influence may have been brought to bear upon the powers that be, because several years into his sentence, Lorcan Bale began to receive a privilege, one that would be considered outrageous in today's prison environment – one that would have turned heads even in the '70s, had it been widely known. About once every two months on a Sunday evening the young convicted child murderer was escorted out of the prison to the nearby Skylon Hotel for a slap-up meal with the family. It was also a treat for the warder escorting the boy; in the '70s dining out in restaurants was enjoyed by a privileged few. There is no record of the conversation, though we can surmise that they dined on '70s fare: prawn marie rose cocktail or tinned orange juice as a starter, chicken à la king with boiled rice as a main and, to complete the evening, the classic black forest gateau. It is hard to imagine what justification was offered for this special treatment. What other inmates thought of it is not recorded.

The rest of Bale's sentence passed unremarkably. Around the

time of his 21st birthday, Lorcan Bale was transferred to Arbour Hill, a medium-security prison whose inmates were mainly men serving long-term sentences. A little over two years later, in September 1980, he began the path to release when he was transferred to the Training Unit, a semi-open prison close to St Patrick's Institution. Here the emphasis was on work and training, a preparation for return to the 'real world', to give young ex-prisoners the skills needed to support themselves without turning back to crime. Three days before Christmas of that same year, Bale walked out of the gates, having been deemed by the justice minister to have served his life sentence. As a lifer, his release had conditions attached, one of which was that he would have to report back to the authorities at regular intervals. In total, Lorcan Bale's actual sentence served for the murder of John Horgan was seven years, six months and one week – almost exactly as long, in fact, as his victim, John Horgan, had lived.

On that chilly December morning, whatever emotions the 23 year old must have felt, one thought must surely have been at the forefront of his mind. It was over. He was free.

# Six

# Nobody Comes into the World this Broken

While researching this book the reactions I witnessed to the story of Lorcan Bale's murder of John Horgan were diverse and yet at the same time predictable: 'shocking', 'appalling' and 'heartbreaking' were words that came up time and again. Other people focused upon the mind of the killer: phrases including, 'he must surely have been deranged', 'pure evil', and 'a mind possessed' were tossed around, delivered not as an opinion but more as a statement of fact. However very few people posed the more probing question: 'Why?' There is no doubt that this was a deliberate, planned act, that there was a sequence of events that culminated in the killing of an innocent child. To attempt to explain why Lorcan Bale went from having a passing interest in the occult to building a satanic shrine in his attic to eventually carrying out what is arguably the most shocking murder in the history of the state, we must soberly examine many issues. This is more than a question about whether the boy was mad or bad, rather, it is about how a person from a stable, comfortable, normal background could go off the rails so completely, how he could be set on such a destructive journey with consequences that resonated far beyond the act itself. Another important question that should be addressed is whether these events would have panned out any differently if they had happened in today's society, in the here and

155

now, and what lessons can be learned from them. Why did no one in authority notice Bale descending from sullen teenager to potential murderer? Is there any action that could have been taken by the adults around him that could have altered the course of events?

The logical point to start at would be Lorcan Bale's early childhood. He was a sickly little boy who suffered from severe asthma from as young as the age of two, and was admitted to hospital several times in his early years. When he was seven, doctors advised that the ailing boy have his tonsils removed in an effort to improve his general health – a widespread practice in the '60s and '70s. Many doctors then believed that removing the tonsils and adenoids was a panacea to solving multiple childhood health problems; the tonsils were viewed as largely useless organs, the removal of which was likely to be of long-term benefit to the patient. During this period of repeated ill-health in his youth, Lorcan attended primary school at Marlborough Street in Dublin city centre, a small school with a focus on the Irish language, which was attached to the Roman Catholic Pro-Cathedral.

At the age of ten, the boy was back in hospital for treatment for a scalded foot. A year later and with the onset of puberty a routine examination at the start of secondary school revealed that he had an undescended testicle. This is a common condition, easily corrected, but one that does require intervention as, left unchecked, it can lead to the growth of tumours or fertility problems in adult life. The operation is known as an orchiopexy: under general anaesthetic a small cut is made in the groin and the testicle is brought down into the scrotum where it is fixed in place with sutures. Typically patients spend a night or two in hospital, and most boys recover fully within a week. However in Lorcan Bale's case, his hospital stay lasted for three weeks.

In January 1970, when he was 12 years old, Lorcan was admitted to Cappagh Hospital in Dublin on the advice of one of the country's most respected paediatricians, Professor Tom Kavanagh, a pioneer in the treatment of young adolescents and a lifelong supporter of homeless charities. Today Cappagh is better known as the National Orthopaedic Hospital, but at the time of Lorcan Bale's admission it was used as a centre for the care of children who had continuing health problems, and could handle up to 164 patients. Because of the long-term nature of the treatments – often counted in years rather than months – a primary school was established within the hospital grounds for the education of the children. It still exists today, served by one full-time teacher. In all, Lorcan Bale spent six months in Cappagh Hospital, a long and likely lonely stretch for the youngster. It was shortly after this time that he showed the first signs of an interest in the occult. Somehow he came across *Man, Myth and Magic*, a periodical made up of numerous articles on very diverse subjects across mythology, alternative and world religions and the supernatural. By today's standards such literature would be unremarkable, if perhaps a little esoteric. There is no doubt that the young Lorcan Bale found it all fascinating.

In the pre-Internet era, in a rigidly Catholic country, such magazines would have been almost impossible to acquire. The list of censored periodicals makes for sober reading. It included *Playboy*, dozens of magazines on the subject of true crime, even the British edition of *The News of the World* (this ban was theoretically still in place at the time of the paper's demise in 2011, though it was not enforced). So how did this sickly boy acquire such a dark reading list? Who supplied him with witchcraft magazines? It is unlikely that he could have sourced them without adult help, and if that is the case, who provided that intervention? And why? While this is the first occasion that we are aware of an emerging interest in the occult, there would be other more sinister signs of adult involvement in what was to become a lethal obsession for Lorcan Bale.

It has to be said there were some happy times at Cappagh Hospital for the sickly youngster; it was in Cappagh where he joined the Catholic Boy Scouts of Ireland and it appeared that, for two years at least, he took a keen interest in scouting. In hospital, he also showed a compassionate side by paying particular attention to disabled patients. But how did this Catholic boy scout, an altar boy, a likeable youngster who was known to help wheelchair-bound friends, end up just a few years later as a cold satanic killer?

Could a deep-seated family resentment have been at the heart of this transformation? Lorcan was the eldest of five children, with three sisters and a brother. His father was deeply conservative, intolerant of the liberal agenda that was slowly enveloping the country. His mother was said to share her husband's views on moral matters, a quiet yet formidable presence in the family. At the time of the murder, Mr Bale told investigators he had spoken to Lorcan a number of times about his surly behaviour and in return the teenager had questioned the validity of the Catholic faith. This must have been difficult for the boy's parents to swallow, religion being at the heart of their family ethos. But despite this Mr Bale took the view that his son was going through a typical teenage rebellious phase. Resentment over the religiosity of the home is certainly worth mentioning, but may not get to the heart of the question of why the boy acted as he did.

Dr Deirdre MacIntyre is a clinical psychologist with 20 years of experience working with parents and children. A specialist in psychology and special needs, she manages an organisation whose aim is to assist children in reaching their full potential through the highest quality continuing professional development. When presented with the facts of John Horgan's murder, Dr MacIntyre's initial reaction was to state that Lorcan Bale showed a high degree of intelligence, was a complex personality and the religiosity of the case meant that it should be unravelled with care. She herself is a mother who grew up not far from Palmerstown in the '70s and remembers a time that was pre-Internet and pre-video. 'So where was he getting the inspiration for all this?' she asked. 'Is there an adult in the background aside from his father?' She believes that the case as presented just does not add up, stating that she knows plenty of people in Ireland who had overbearing, ultra right-wing, Catholic fathers, yet none of them grew up to be violent. Her argument is validated by the fact that Lorcan's four siblings had the same parents, yet grew into perfectly normal, balanced teenagers and adults; indeed today they are well-liked and highly regarded, each accomplished in their own fields. Her opening salvo concluded with a telling observation. 'There has to be a missing link,' she said quietly. 'Nobody comes into the world this broken. It is learned.'

Let us assume that Lorcan Bale did not learn this behaviour from his father. There is no evidence to suggest that Kenneth Bale is anything but a victim in this sorry affair. In any event, Mr Bale has been dead for over 25 years so cannot add anything more to this story than we already know. If he were still alive, it would be revealing to ask why he knew so little about his son's descent into the occult. With nine people living in the house – the Bale parents, five children and Mrs Bale's parents – how did he not know that his son had built an elaborate satanic shrine in the roof space? The shrine must have taken months to construct, a private space complete with altar, chalice, Ouija board, strange powders, a specially constructed trap door and even its own electric light supply.

We are sure that Lorcan and his father did not see eye to eye on most matters, and it is certainly credible that the teenager's anger against his father was way beyond adolescent squabbling, indeed the rage that he demonstrated on that June afternoon was utterly primeval. While the satanic ceremony in the attic of the Bale house was directed towards the devil, Lorcan Bale may well have been crucifying his ultra-religious father in his own mind, in what could be described as the ultimate anti-father act, an attack on his father's beliefs. In doing what he did, Lorcan found the most extreme way to reject, destroy and sully all that his family held dear.

So if not from his father, even as a warning about the evil, anti-Christian forces existing in the world, where did the teenager gain knowledge of the occult? Could it have been the satanic group in

County Meath that he spoke about to his school friend Lorcan Conroy? The same group that he might have visited to attend a sexual initiation ceremony during four days of disappearance at the winter solstice of 1972. A few of those who knew him in the years following the murder believe that while he acted alone, the killing must have been a 'joint venture'. This idea arises because there is a strong belief that it is simply not feasible for a teenager to dream up such an elaborate plan on their own, rather it is speculated that Bale was nurtured and groomed by adults, occult obsessives who gave this sickly vulnerable boy books that – knowingly or unknowingly – would give his actions an intellectual justification and sow the seeds for his later murderous behaviour.

Between the killing and the trial, Lorcan Bale spent five months on remand in St Patrick's Institution facing a charge of murder. In that time, he came into contact with a wide range of people including police, prison officers, other prisoners, psychologists, psychiatrists and his legal team, all in their own different ways enquiring about why he had carried out such an appalling act. It was essential that an accurate assessment of Bale's mental state was established before the trial, and that duty fell primarily to two of the country's most gifted minds, clinical psychologist Maureen Gaffney and psychiatrist Dr Brian McCaffrey. The pair had several sessions with the accused and after a period of months produced a report that was made available to the trial judge, Mr Justice Kenny. That report is covered by client patient confidentiality and so is not in the public domain; however, because Lorcan Bale made a guilty plea, we can infer at least that he was judged fit to stand trial, that the mental health professionals declared that he was not suffering from mental illness. In their professional opinion, and this is an extreme over-simplification, his actions may have been heartless, cruel and deliberate, but he certainly was not insane.

In coming to this conclusion, there were legal guidelines to consider. If a similar case were to happen today, the first place to seek such guidance is the Criminal Law (Insanity) Act 2006. This gives a clear steer on several important issues relating to the trial of a person who may be suffering from mental illness, including whether a person is fit to be tried, diminished responsibility, temporary release and other matters. It was a long overdue and welcome piece of legislation; previously such decisions were based on laws that owe more to the legal values and psychiatric knowledge of the Victorian era than any of the advances of understanding made in the twentieth century. Not only that, but the language used was wildly out of date and at times offensive – at the time of Lorcan Bale's trial, two laws still on the statute books were the Criminal Lunatics Act 1800 and the Trial of Lunatics Act 1883, both now fully repealed.

Today's updated legislation, The Criminal Law (Insanity) Act 2006 has clear guidance about whether a person is capable of being tried before a court of law. In 1973, when considering the Bale cause, broadly similar criteria would have been followed.

> An accused person shall be deemed unfit to be tried if he or she is unable by reason of mental disorder to understand the nature or course of the proceedings so as to -
> (a) plead to the charge,
> (b) instruct a legal representative,
> (c) in the case of an indictable offence which may be tried summarily, elect for a trial by jury,
> (d) make a proper defence,
> (e) in the case of a trial by jury, challenge a juror to whom he or she might wish to object, or
> (f) understand the evidence.

The Act defines 'mental disorder' as including 'mental illness, mental disability, dementia or any other disease of the mind but does not include intoxication'.

Stripping back the wordy legal language, you could argue that the test as to whether a person is fit for trial should be stiffer. Boiling down the rules as they exist, the accused has simply to understand what is going on and be aware of the charges against them, follow the nature of the proceedings, instruct a lawyer and so on. Some legal experts have suggested that fitness for trial should have broader criteria, including a measure of the accused's intellectual ability. Darius Whelan, law lecturer at University College, Cork and president of the Irish Mental Health Lawyers Association has questioned the efficacy of the system.

> Is it really sufficient that a person may be tried on a very serious criminal charge on the basis that he or she understands what is going on?
>
> It has been persuasively argued elsewhere that the law should require a person to have 'decisional capacity' so that they can be a true participant in the process.

In examining Lorcan Bale's state of mind to assess whether he would be fit to plead, what telltale signs might the experts have been seeking? Firstly they would have asked themselves if the teenager was suffering from a form of psychosis, a severe mental disorder in which thought and emotions are so impaired that victims entirely lose touch with objective reality. Typically psychotic personalities are delusional, and though they are not necessarily actively malicious, they can cause harm to others as they react to these delusions. Psychosis can be present in types of schizophrenia, when patients hear voices or believe that their actions are being controlled by an external power. Clinical psychologist Dr Deirdre MacIntyre believes the evidence of psychosis exhibited by Bale is minimal, due to the fact that his actions were not impulsive.

> The teenager was unlikely to have been psychotic as he was organised cognitively. The level of organisation shows that he could function clearly, that he could hold it together. He had the site pre-chosen, he had the excuse, he had the sack, the weapon – all suggesting a psychopathic picture rather than a psychotic one.

162

So if he were not psychotic, is it more likely that Bale was in some way psychopathic – by definition a person suffering from a chronic mental disorder with abnormal or violent social behaviour? A key phrase that comes up time and again when describing psychopathic behaviour is a 'lack of empathy'. Most of us, when we see a man hit his thumb with a hammer, wince in sympathy, or at the conclusion of a heartbreaking film, feel tears welling up in our eyes. When we perceive others to be in pain, we suffer ourselves, like a little echo of the feelings we observe. Similarly through empathy yawning becomes contagious and a group of gigglers cannot stop laughing. But a psychopath does not possess this particular tangle of neural wiring; to them the sight of another's pain or discomfort is more likely to seem amusing, if anything, a departure from the impassive or implacable norm. Sometimes the psychopath enjoys the suffering of others enough to actively seek it out, and this is where many young killers begin.

In criminal psychology, the torturing of animals is seen as one of the two very big warning signs, alongside starting fires. There is clear evidence that Lorcan Bale captured and killed animals for his own satisfaction. He laid traps for rats, their bodies were quickly decomposed in a specially constructed lime pit, and he made necklaces from rats' skulls. His cruel behaviour towards animals went further: he killed a neighbour's dog by connecting a cord around its neck, attaching the rope and making the unfortunate animal run. He also tried and failed to kill a cat that proved too agile and aggressive for the boy. The following day he turned up at school with his face covered in scratches. Mice belonging to some of Hollyville's younger residents disappeared; Bale told a teenager living nearby how easy it would be to steal the pet rabbits from the Dempster family. Subsequently the rabbits went missing.

But before glibly attaching a psychopathic label to the teenager, it is important to momentarily step back. When a child is under 18, psychiatrists will not diagnose psychopathic behaviour. Rather they speak of a child suffering from a 'conduct disorder'. Put simply, Lorcan Bale could not have been a psychopath as he was too young for such a diagnosis. Teenagers can exhibit anti-social behaviour in adolescence and subsequently grow out of it. The American Psychiatric Association has carried out a great deal of work in this area and has published a document that lists the diagnostic criteria for a conduct disorder. Their definition of conduct disorder in young people makes for interesting reading:

CONDUCT DISORDER: A repetitive and persistent pattern of behaviour in which the basic rights of others or major age-appropriate societal norms or rules are violated, as manifested by the presence of three (or more) of the following criteria in the past 12 months, with at least one criterion present in the past six months:

Aggression to people and/or animals

1. Often bullies, threatens or intimidates others.
2. Often initiates physical fights.
3. Has used a weapon that can cause serious physical harm to others (e.g., a bat, brick, broken bottle, knife, gun).
4. Has been physically cruel to people.
5. Has been physically cruel to animals.
6. Has stolen while confronting a victim (e.g., mugging, purse snatching, extortion, armed robbery).
7. Has forced someone into sexual activity.

There are parallels between John Horgan's murder and a case in the United States that was to occur twenty years later, in 1993, with the discovery of two bodies found on a country road in Ellis County, Texas. This was a grisly murder of two young teens: a fourteen-year-old boy Brian King had been shot, while the other victim, thirteen-year-old Christina Benjamin had been raped, mutilated and dismembered – her head and hands were both missing from the murder scene. The killer, Jason Massey, was eventually apprehended and under police questioning he revealed that his ambition was to be known as the worst serial killer that ever stalked the state of Texas. He too had a history of torturing animals, he had stalked another young woman without killing her, and he hero-worshipped notorious killers such as Ted Bundy, Charles Manson, and Henry Lee Lucas. At the age of nine he killed his first cat. Over the years dozens more met the same fate, along with many dogs and even half a dozen cows. Investigators discovered a long list of potential victims as well as a personal diary that was filled with fantasies of raping, torturing, and cannibalising women. Like Lorcan Bale, Jason Massey was a loner who spoke of serving a 'master' who gave him knowledge and power. There are other parallels: Massey was obsessed with bringing his victims under his control and having their dead bodies in his possession. After almost eight years on death row, Massey was executed by lethal injection in 2001.

While Lorcan Bale was awaiting trial, the psychiatrist tasked with examining him was Dr Brian McCaffrey. McCaffrey is now aged 76 and has 50 years of medical practice under his belt. Patient confidentiality prevented him from discussing the Bale case, however he did agree to speak in general terms about his methods, and this in itself gives insights into how the sessions with the Dublin teenager may have been structured. Dr McCaffrey trained initially at St Brendan's, a large hospital treating mental-health conditions sited north of Dublin, before moving to Glasgow, where he was mentored by Ian Hunter Gillies, a highly regarded forensic psychiatrist and an authority on murder in the west of Scotland. Two postings in the United States followed where the young Irish doctor learned a great deal about schizophrenia. He recalls one patient who was virtually demented, drooling and refusing to talk. In their sessions, the patient appeared to regress into the time he was carried in his mother's womb and from that point made substantial progress. He and others like him responded well to treatment, one even becoming a top graduate engineer.

Returning to Dublin as a clinical director at St Brendan's, Dr McCaffrey was asked to assist in some court evaluation work and developed a flair for the job. His style was to encourage patients to get as comfortable and relaxed as possible, not quizzing or judging them, but rather adopting a listening approach to allow them to state whatever happened to be on their mind at that time. 'To my own surprise, I found that I was very comfortable with adult males who were very violent and very dangerous. I just clicked with them,' the psychiatrist recalled.

Very gradually, he would enquire about their relationship history, their parents, partners and children. Alcoholism in the family was a recurring theme, as was sexual abuse.

> Childhood can be a very revealing issue, not just physical or sexual abuse, but also the effect of child play with siblings. Other factors that can help make an assessment could include academic record and school experiences such as participation in sports.
>
> I never jump in asking blunt questions like 'Are you hearing voices?' There are more subtle ways like talking about trust and fears.

Several of Dr McCaffrey's remand prisoners under his assessment turned out to be psychotic and the signs of psychosis appeared not in an instant, but gradually over time. If the patient felt that there were voices present in their mind, they could face questions such as 'What are the voices saying?' 'Are they speaking in English?' or 'Are they using obscene words?' Over the years, the doctor carried out hundreds of sessions, developing an expertise in the human experience of trauma, of violent teachers, abusive parents, even the trauma of army soldiers having witnessed atrocities in battle.

> When I have a criminal case for assessment, I study the Book of Evidence and with the permission of the accused – who to me is also a client – I talk to significant people in their lives, such as parents, siblings and partners. More often than not,

> the client would deny me this permission and I would have to
> proceed with the client alone. To make an assessment, I push
> to get as much time as possible, certainly months not weeks.

Pausing to pour another cup of strong tea, he added, 'I really don't like rushing.'

Five months after the killing, Lorcan Bale was in court facing a charge of murder. The reports that had been carefully prepared by clinical psychologist Maureen Gaffney and psychiatrist Dr Brian McCaffrey were praised for their content, not just by the judge Mr Justice Kenny but also by Lorcan Bale's barrister Seamus Sorahan, Senior Counsel. Their content, however, remains confidential. At the trial, the defendant's demeanour was said to be expressionless. Some who were there saw this as a lack of remorse, and described him as 'evil', a term which can mean different things to different people but is a fairly common description for one who murders for pleasure and feels no guilt about his actions. Yet some of those who knew Lorcan Bale at the time did not see him as evil, despite their knowledge of what he had done. They found him to be an engaging and likeable young man, neither mad nor bad. When it comes down to it, someone needs to do something very bad to be considered 'evil', but crucially, they must be *hated for what they did*. It is your hate for someone that defines them as 'evil' in your mind, not your judgement. That is why the people who liked Lorcan Bale do not think he was evil. And why, in the United States, serial killers on death row still get visits from their mothers.

A better question than asking if Lorcan Bale was 'evil' would be to ask whether he was a real satanist following a dangerous spiritual belief system, or if he was using this so-called religion as a cover, an excuse to indulge the darker impulses that have no place in conventional morality? True satanists – men and women who believe in the Christian Devil and choose to worship him as a deity – are actually quite rare. Satanism is an inversion and deliberate parody of Catholicism, not a developed spirituality; its rituals and theology are either defined by or lifted wholesale from the

Christianity it professes to reject. As such, it is an excellent way for those angry with the religion to rebel without ever truly challenging their own beliefs, but it does not lend itself to stable long-term practice. The vast majority of those who call themselves satanists are in fact angry or disturbed young people who are drawn by the promise of sex or violence or being granted powers that they can use against others. For them, satanism is an excuse to do things they know to be wrong, and, sometimes, a force to blame when they get caught.

Lorcan Bale's history of torturing animals is a clear sign of a lack of empathy. An offender who feels little guilt over their crime can easily rationalise their own anti-social behaviour, by saying to themselves that their actions were simply an extension of their spiritual beliefs. But as an ordinary Irish teenager, he would surely have had his own concerns about the enormity of what he had done and how, if at all, he was going to get away with it. A practicing Christian cannot legitimately pray to God for success in an action that would be in direct contravention of His Commandments; it would be absurd to seek divine intervention to allow an offender to get away with murder. But on the other hand, a negative spiritual belief system, such as a professed satanic creed, might have fulfilled Bale's human need for intervention from a power greater than himself.

One of the world's leading authorities on murder linked to the occult is Jacob V. Lanning, formerly Supervisory Special Agent at the Behavioral Science Unit within the National Center for the Analysis of Violent Crime – a specialist division of the FBI in Virginia. Having analysed hundreds of cases from child abuse with occult factors to satanic murder, Lanning's view is clear.

> For those who know anything about criminology, one of the oldest theories of crime is demonology: the Devil makes you do it. This makes it even easier to deal with the child molester who is the 'pillar of the community'. It is not his fault; it is not our fault. There is no way we could have known; the

Devil made him do it. This explanation has tremendous appeal because, like 'stranger danger', it presents the clear-cut, black-and-white struggle between good and evil as the explanation for child abduction, exploitation, and abuse.

So if the Devil did not make him do it, there are only two options left: either Bale decided entirely independently to take the life of the little boy next door, or he did so having been brainwashed by adults. The complication with this case is the religiosity that surrounds it – the shrine, the chalice and the cruciform manner in which the body was discovered. Because of the apparently demonic circumstances, it is inevitably difficult to separate out murder from so-called satanic murder. Jacob Lanning of the FBI believes that occult evidence can on occasions mask the true picture.

> All of this is complicated by the fact that almost any discussion of satanism and the occult is interpreted in the light of the religious beliefs of those in the audience. Faith, not logic and reason, governs the religious beliefs of most people. As a result, some normally sceptical law enforcement officers accept the information disseminated without critically evaluating it or questioning the sources.

For some, there is no such thing as satanism, only crimes and the rituals surrounding them. But for others the dangers surrounding dark demonic forces are very real. Bill Brophy grew up near Palmerstown in the '70s and is now a police officer in the UK. Just like almost everyone else in Ireland, Brophy was raised a Catholic, never missed Sunday Mass, and was given a solid spiritual grounding by the Vincentian monks at Castleknock College. As a young adult, he gradually drifted away from the church until, on a sporting trip to Wales, he underwent a religious conversion at a church service in the city of Cardiff. He remembers the murder of John Horgan well, mostly because the case was a huge mystery to the local community. Back in the '70s, he recalls, there was a widespread interest in the occult, partly because of the influence of such films as *The Omen* (1976) and *The Exorcist* (1973). With this backdrop, a widespread belief that Lorcan Bale was a member of a satanic cult developed in the area.

'I certainly believed that,' stated Brophy. 'After all, who influenced him and where did he get the materials such as the Ouija board?' He goes further, calling upon his personal beliefs as an evangelical Christian. 'I believe absolutely that Lorcan Bale was a victim of demonic possession. I say this not just because of his beliefs, but due to the tools of his trade. Clearly he was reading books about the occult; he has to have been influenced by adults, perhaps with the promise of sex but most of all I would have huge concerns about his use of the Ouija board.' Brophy feels strongly that these are dangerous instruments, particularly in the hands of a vulnerable sickly teenager, as, he believes, they force you to empty your mind and to open up to outside forces.

'When the two Lorcans had that séance in the attic,' observed Officer Brophy, 'I don't believe they were communicating with a dead boy, but rather they were in touch with a demon that was taking on the persona of familiar spirits recently departed.' In conclusion, he added, 'All this says to me that Lorcan Bale was definitely demon possessed and influenced by powers greater than himself.'

Father Clement Keane, the Catholic priest and exorcist who examined the crucifix found in the attic of the Horgan house, is more circumspect.

'All the outward signs state that Lorcan Bale was possessed; a friend who is a nun wanted to see him when he was in St Patrick's Institution, but was forbidden from doing so. However without having examined him, I cannot say for certain. His actions can quite easily be accounted for without invoking a spiritual explanation. Just think of the trauma that Lorcan suffered in his early life. Consider the fact that he spent a long time alone in hospital – so did he react badly to separation from his family, making him feel rejected, losing self esteem, even questioning his own identity and thus allowing an inner rage to take hold?'

'So in your opinion, Lorcan Bale's actions have no spiritual dimension and are simply those of a murderer?' I asked.

'Not necessarily. Let's assume for the sake of argument there was a spirit oppressing him. The first question you have to ask is, "Where was the opening that allowed the spirit to enter his mind?" A spirit can exploit a psychic wound, an injury triggered by a traumatic event like separation anxiety, but could include getting involved in the occult. Once you open your mind up to a spirit, you can become very vulnerable. The person and the spirit oppressing him join in consent together, they're in partnership together. The next stage is the gaining of power, at this time he also can become a very efficient liar.'

Father Clement paused for a moment to choose his words. 'For Lorcan Bale, this may have been the ultimate power trip. The killing of this little boy and the way his body was displayed may have been profoundly symbolic. Don't forget the child had just received his first Holy Communion, and Bale may well have said to himself, "I will display power over you. I will kill you off." It was terribly, terribly malicious.'

There is an entirely contrary view: that Bale might have categorised his own actions as being those of a satanist, but in truth he was a boy who was simply a dabbler in the occult.

The expert from the National Center for the Analysis of Violent Crime, the FBI's Jacob Lanning, is convinced that satanic or occult practices can be used by an offender as a mechanism to facilitate a clear criminal objective. 'For these practitioners there is little or no spiritual motivation' says Lanning.

> They may mix satanism, witchcraft, paganism, and any aspects of the occult to suit their purposes. Symbols mean whatever they want them or believe them to mean. Molesters, rapists, drug dealers, and murderers may dabble in the occult and may even commit their crimes in a ceremonial or ritualistic way. This category has the potential to be the most dangerous,

and most 'satanic' killers fall into this category. Their involvement in satanism and the occult is a symptom of a problem, and a rationalisation and justification of antisocial behaviour.

Having established the detail of the crime and made an effort to get into the mind of the killer, the next logical question to ask is, 'Could this murder have been prevented, and if so what can now be done to avoid a similar attack in the future?' To have averted the murder, persons in authority would have had to know that Lorcan Bale had the potential to be a killer. Putting aside crimes of passion, murder tends to occur at the end of a sliding scale: verbal abuse, petty crime, assault, grievous bodily harm, attempted murder and eventually murder. However while this case did follow this pattern, starting with Bale's frequent fights with other teenagers, going on to his break-in and theft of money from his school, and his cruel treatment of animals, none of this was known to the Gardaí, the Irish police force. He had no documented history of violence towards children, or to anyone for that matter. So it would be unfair and inappropriate to say that the police could have done more; until the day of the murder, he was never on their radar.

Hours before he snuffed out the life of the little boy, Lorcan Bale mentioned to his school friend Lorcan Conroy that he was thinking of killing the boy next door. Conroy had heard many fanciful ramblings from Bale over the years, and dismissed it as yet another nonsensical boast from a teenager with a long history of telling tall tales. That inaction has haunted Conroy throughout his adult life. But realistically, what else could he have done? He had no reason to believe the event would actually occur, but if he had, for instance, mentioned it to his parents, would they have listened? Would the police? Given the fact that Lorcan Bale had no prior criminal record, no documented history of violence, it is highly unlikely any action would have been taken. All his life, Conroy has battled with the fact that he alone had a foretaste of his classmate's intent that day and yet Bale's murderous path went unhindered.

With police intervention a non-starter, and any cries from Lorcan Conroy unlikely to be taken seriously, could either Lorcan Bale's parents or his school have done more to put a stop to his destructive journey? Any right-thinking person would agree that the teenager should have been undergoing some form of counselling at that time, such was his bizarre behaviour. In particular the killing and torturing of animals should have triggered alarm bells that would have been heard across the city. However, when you gather the evidence and interview his contemporaries, it becomes quickly clear that the people who knew most about the animal sacrifices were themselves children. Today youngsters making out of the ordinary claims tend to get a fair hearing from adults, but in the '70s the rule of children being 'seen but not heard' remained firmly in place. The boys and girls who were aware of Bale's disturbing behaviour towards animals are unlikely to have recognised that this was potentially a precursor to more violent behaviour. We know that Lorcan Bale had a frosty relationship with his father and did not get on particularly well with his siblings, notably with his sisters. So it is fair to surmise that Mr and Mrs Bale believed that their eldest son was a surly, obstinate, rude and moody teenager, but if they had such poor communication with the boy, then it is highly unlikely that they could ever have suspected that Lorcan had within him the growing potential to become a child killer.

So if not at home, could his predisposition to violence have been picked up at school? In '70s Ireland, most likely not. Despite his high IQ, Bale's schooling was marked by a failing academic record, occasional truanting, unconventional dress, lack of interest in sport and solitary behaviour. Put together they added up to very little, that is, if no serious effort were made to delve into the personality of the boy. Coláiste Mhuire is proud of its academic tradition: current alumnae include the Lord Mayor of Dublin, Gerry Breen; Anglo-Irish Bank Chairman, Alan Dukes; and actor Brian McGrath among other respected Irish figures. Excellence in the examination hall and on the sports field were greatly encouraged. However several former pupils have said that less academic or sporty types were largely left to their own devices.

Lorcan Bale slipped through a net that was full of holes, though today it is doubtful that this boy would have been similarly ignored. With the rigorous pastoral care schemes that exist in modern schools, it is highly probable that he would have been seen by an educational psychologist, who in turn would more than likely have referred him to a child psychiatrist. Analysing the mind of a young person suffering from a personality disorder has come a long way in recent years; perhaps one of the most significant milestones has been the work of Dr Robert D. Hare, a Canadian researcher renowned in the field of criminal psychology. Hare developed and revised the Psychopathy Checklist, used to diagnose cases of psychopathy and a useful tool for predicting the likelihood of violent behaviour. This tool is a clinical rating scale where the scores are added up and used to predict risk for criminal re-offence and probability of rehabilitation.

The first personality traits a psychiatrist would seek using Dr Hare's method would be signs of 'aggressive narcissism'. These include glibness or superficial charm, a grandiose sense of self-worth, pathological lying, being cunning or manipulative, showing a lack of remorse or guilt, displaying a shallow nature where genuine emotion is short-lived and egocentric, being callous with a lack of empathy and failure to accept responsibility for their own actions.

All this remains a long way from the notion of pre-crime as put forward in the futuristic movie *Minority Report* (2002), in which law enforcement officers arrest potential criminals before they get an opportunity to commit crimes. Almost 40 years ago, when Lorcan Bale showed his first inklings of destructive behaviour, there were simply not the structures in place to recognise him for what he was.

# SEVEN

## The 38-Year Inquest

Tuesday, 24 May 2011. The Maldron Hotel, Tallaght, County Dublin.

On this bright windy morning, a small group of people smartly-dressed in business suits gathered together for a highly unusual event, one that passed by the dozens of guests casually coming and going from this pleasant, three-star hotel. The business suited group might have been here for any number of reasons – a meeting, a sales seminar or any one of the conferences for which the Maldron has made its name. However, a discreet word at the reception desk would reveal that on this mid-week morning, the conference room had been booked by the Dublin County Coroner, who was a regular corporate customer of the Maldron. That morning, he would be holding an inquest into the death of a little boy, a tragedy long forgotten to all but a few. The coroner, his administrative team, a select group of witnesses, Garda officers and a tiny posse of curious journalists were quietly preparing for the opening of proceedings, each in their different ways: some checking yellowing folders, seeking an intermittent Wi-Fi signal, surmising who else had turned up for this event; others were focused on more mundane morning routines – ordering good strong coffee, grabbing a quick cigarette, or ploughing through endless voicemails.

They were all here to confirm a fact that each of them already knew: the cause of death of John Joseph Horgan almost exactly

175

38 years earlier. For reasons that, at that point, were unknown to most in the room, the inquest into the death of the boy back in 1973 had never been properly concluded. The other consequences of that awful day – the funeral of little John and the punishment of his killer – were long since over, but due to one small oversight the case had not been properly, formally closed. It had languished for the past 38 years in a legal and administrative limbo. On that muggy Tuesday morning, Dr Kieran Geraghty, Coroner for the County of Dublin, was to be the man to finally put the case to rest, almost four decades after it was first opened.

In Ireland, as in the UK, an inquest is a formal public enquiry, the purpose of which is to discover the reasons behind a sudden, unexplained or violent death. There is no judge, instead the proceedings are presided over by the coroner, a specialist who must either be a qualified lawyer or a registered doctor. Sometimes, but not always, there is a jury who will hear the evidence, deliberate in confidence and in their own time come to a verdict. Death does not always result in the deceased's final moments being debated at an inquest. Indeed, if the cause of death can be clearly ascertained at a post-mortem, then there is generally no need for an inquest. The word itself is a clue to its exact purpose: in Old French the word 'enqueste' was used to describe an enquiry. By the late thirteenth century, the term 'an-queste' was a well-established way of referring to a legal or judicial inquiry in which the cause of death was a mystery. For only upon solving the mystery and firmly establishing the cause of death could lessons be learned to prevent such fatalities from happening again.

An inquest is, however, very different to a trial. Where a trial is a formal examination of evidence by a judge, typically before a jury, in order to decide guilt in a case of criminal or civil proceedings, an inquest aims to establish the essential facts of the death – typically, where the person died and, most importantly, how the death occurred. At an inquest no criminal or civil liability is determined, nor is a person ever found guilty or innocent. All that may come later. There is another key difference between an inquest and a criminal trial: the entire paperwork – depositions, post-mortem reports and verdict records – are preserved by the coroner and in due course are made available to any member of the public who is interested enough to hunt through the records. The Irish inquest rules are laid down by the Coroners Act 1962, a weighty tome that runs to dozens of pages, but is neatly summed up by Section 17, which reads:

> Subject to the provisions of this Act, where a coroner is informed that the body of a deceased person is lying within his district, it shall be the duty of the coroner to hold an inquest in relation to the death of that person if he is of opinion that the death may have occurred in a violent or unnatural manner, or suddenly and from unknown causes or in a place or in circumstances which, under provisions in that behalf contained in any other enactment, require that an inquest should be held.

Normally the coroner needs time to gather the facts to present before the jury and so, under usual circumstances, an inquest will not be convened until at least six weeks after the person's death. Thankfully this does not mean that a funeral has to be delayed for months; normally a post-mortem is held, the findings recorded and the body released to the family for burial or cremation within a matter of days.

Often witnesses are called; their testimony regarding the circumstances and possible cause of death is sworn on oath. Typically witnesses are people who were present at a road traffic accident, or were involved in fighting a house fire, or perhaps police officers attending the scene of an as-yet-unexplained fatality. It is the coroner and the coroner alone who decides which witnesses should give evidence at the inquest as well as the order in which they should give their evidence. To help the jury come to a just decision, every effort is made to present the evidence in the order in which it occurred. In other words, there should be a logical sequence for the subject of the inquest from life to death. The main medical witness is almost always the pathologist who carried out the post-mortem, the result of which normally establishes the medical cause of death.

When all the evidence is heard, the jury – if there is one – delivers its verdict. Unlike trial juries where twelve men or women, good and true, must judge the accused, an Irish inquest jury can have as few as six members, though in practice the authorities make every effort to muscle in as close to twelve as possible. A jury is only required in certain specialist circumstances, including if:

The death is due to murder, manslaughter or infanticide

The death took place in prison

The death was caused by an accident, poisoning or a disease requiring notification to a government department or inspector

The death was caused by a road traffic accident

The death occurred in circumstances, which if they continued or recurred would endanger the health or safety of a member(s) of the public

The coroner considers that a jury is necessary.

Inquests are usually held in a courthouse. Sometimes local halls or hotels with decent conference facilities, like the Maldron in Tallaght, are used. The family of the dead person have every right to be there, and very often attend if only to seek a sense of closure. However, there is no compulsion on the family to attend and many do not, the experience often being simply too painful to revisit. When families do sit in on an inquest, they may have a lawyer with them to explain the proceedings and to take accurate notes, but this is rarely necessary unless the family members themselves are potentially the subject of legal action. Some rules governing inquests allow no flexibility at all, including the edict that if a death is due to unnatural causes, an inquest must be held, by law.

An inquest will confirm the identity of the victim. In most cases identification will be provided by a relative or close friend who will have previously seen the body, but in cases where the body is not readily recognisable – such as death by fire or where the remains have been badly decomposed – then specialists may provide identification through dental records, DNA matching or other means. If the jury at the inquest cannot agree on the cause of death, the coroner has a number of options: he or she can either accept the majority decision of the jury or, if the decision is tied, send the jury home and hold a new inquest. When all is done, the jury will confirm the identity of the dead person, and also where, when and, most importantly, how the death occurred. Armed with this information, the coroner will pronounce his verdict – though in jury cases it is they who make this announcement – which can range from 'accidental death' to 'misadventure', 'suicide', an 'open verdict', 'natural causes' and, in cases where murder or manslaughter has occurred, a verdict of 'unlawful killing' can be announced. Occasionally, there are lessons to be learned, and in such cases the coroner can issue recommendations so that other families are less likely to find themselves one day in a coroner's court pondering what might have happened had circumstances been different.

Unlike trials involving juveniles, or the proceedings of family law courts, all inquests held in Ireland are conducted in public and anyone may attend. In practice, they are normally very sad procedural affairs and rarely attract much passing traffic, just the curious or the plain nosy. However a common feature is that in the back row of the public gallery will be found a reporter from a local regional newspaper, hopeful for any titbit that can become a story of local or national interest. The reporter's job in a regional coroner's court is a lonely one; few inquests make it to even the middle pages of a daily newspaper.

In Ireland, newspaper editors and coroners alike are highly sensitive to the very real tragedies that run hand in glove with many inquests. Unlike their counterparts in other countries, there is a culture of holding back the blood and gore, a recognition that the proceedings are real enquiries into the tragic deaths of real people, so in deference to the sensitivities of the grieving family, certain details are sometimes withheld. If, for example, there is an inquest into a suicide, the existence of a suicide note may be acknowledged, but its wording may be skirted over. Ireland in the '70s was a place where ghastly business involving Irish people was not readily discussed in the open. While people were aware that dreadful happenings, up to and including murder, did take place, it was felt that there was a time and a place to discuss such deeds. A coroner's court was appropriate, being an official body, as was a discussion among friends, or a one-to-one in the confessional, but the pages of a newspaper were deemed to be too open, too crass. Put simply, Irish people until quite recently did not wash their dirty linen in public.

The very last act of an inquest is always for the coroner to issue a death certificate so that the death can be formally registered. It was the failure of the 1973 inquest in this regard that brought together the suited men and women to the Maldron Hotel in Tallaght, County Dublin, on that Tuesday morning, a full 38 years after John Horgan had died.

The 2011 inquest was the result of an administrative accident. In researching this book and the circumstances surrounding the death of John Horgan, I drew upon a wide range of sources. With virtually no mention of the case online, it was essential to source any written documentation available. The search began at Ireland's General Register Office, a public research facility where the records of all the nation's births, deaths and marriages are kept. Writing a non-fiction book might be said to be akin to piecing together a jigsaw, except there is no picture to guide you, and the box is unlikely to contain more than a few pieces. However, for 20 euro per day, anyone can begin to find some of the pieces of a genealogical puzzle: birth indexes are held in huge leather-bound red books, marriage records in green, while – appropriately – the death books are clad in black.

It took a day to find the public records of people associated with this book, those at the centre of events, whose certificates would occasionally reveal their own stories. John Horgan's birth certificate told us that he was born in Mount Carmel Hospital, and the paperwork revealed that his parents were married in the village of Hackettstown in County Carlow. Lorcan Bale's birth certificate and those of his siblings were in Irish, hardly surprising given the family background. There can be other eye-opening moments in the documentation, such as the mistake made in Lorcan Bale's younger brother's birth certificate where the incorrect date was entered; his mother had to return weeks later and make a sworn declaration to correct it. But one document appeared to be missing: the death certificate for the murder victim, young John Horgan. A trawl through the records of 1973 revealed that 22 Horgans passed away that year but, according to the records, John was not among their number. It would be unusual for a death certificate to be held back for a period of months, but given the fact that there were criminal proceedings attached to the case – the trial took place in November 1973, five months after the murder – could it be that the death certificate was recorded in 1974? A search through the black books for 1974 and 1975 also uncovered nothing. The archive staff found the absence baffling, especially given that the death was the homicide of a child, and given that professionals who would routinely issue this vital document were involved in the inquest.

Perhaps there had been an inquest, but for some reason a death certificate was never issued? It was a long shot but worth a trip to the National Archives in Dublin, where records for all inquests of that period are held. The names and basic information are etched in handwritten directories, each with their own reference number. Finding the right reference number should directly lead the researcher to the complete inquest file. This time the search did bear fruit. After leafing through dozens of dusty volumes, one page in a heavy leather book with a frayed cover pointed to the case. Sandwiched between listings for the inquest into the death of Dr Dennis O'Farrell (cardiorespiratory failure as a result of a road traffic accident) and Minne Walsh (drowning) were the words:

> John Horgan
> Address: 6 Hollyville, Lucan Road, Palmerstown
> Date of inquest: 11/7/73 – adjourned
> Where held: City Morgue, Store Street
> Verdict: Fracture of the skull, contusion & laceration of the
>     brain – result of blunt force injury to the back of head.

So there had been an inquest, but it had been adjourned. The full file would surely reveal the reason why. A few days later, and after some difficulty in locating it, a small brown folder was produced from somewhere in the bowels of the National Archives. The papers inside – many original documents – revealed important first-hand information, much of which is contained in this book. There are several Garda documents, phone logs and, crucially, a letter from a Garda, Sergeant Patrick McGirr, to the Dublin County Coroner, Dr Bartley Sheehan. The letter details how the boy was first reported missing, a call that led to an immediate police response.

> A party of Gardai under direction of Inspector John J. White, Clondalkin Station, commenced a search of the area surrounding the missing boy's home. The boy had last been in the company of one Lorcan Bale, 16½ years, 7 Hollyville, Palmerstown, a near neighbour. The investigating Gardai questioned the latter and, after some time, he led them to the attic of his home at No 7, Hollyville, where the missing boy was found dead, tied in a spread-eagled fashion on the rafters at approximately 11pm on 14.6.73.

The letter goes on to explain to the coroner the circumstances in which they believed the boy had died.

Apparently Deceased was left in care of the Bale family on the day of 14th June 1973 while his parents were absent from home. Lorcan Bale invited the child out into a field behind his house to look for rabbits. He clubbed the deceased from behind as he was looking at a rabbit hole, which he, Bale, had pointed out to him. Subsequently he removed the body to the attic of his home in a sack.

The letter concludes with medical observations and a line about the suspect.

The Deceased was pronounced dead on examination in attic at No 7, Hollyville by Doctor T.B. Sherry, 11 Palmerstown Avenue, Palmerstown, Dublin 20. Lorcan Bale, as above, is at present in Lucan Garda Station. On your instructions the body is being removed to City Morgue where Dr M. Hickey, State Pathologist, will carry out P.M. [post-mortem] after identification.

Underneath the letter was a sworn statement, a deposition made by the victim's aunt, Eileen Horgan, a district nurse living in Clontarf, a coastal suburb of north Dublin. The statement, which is signed in her own hand, was made in the Dublin city morgue on 15 June 1973, the day after the boy's death. It is simple, to the point and desperately sad:

On the 15th of June 1973, I was shown the body of a young boy at the City Morgue, Store Street, Dublin. I identified the body as that of my nephew John Horgan, 6 Hollyville, Lucan Road, Palmerstown, Co. Dublin. He was born on 27th August 1965. I last saw him alive on (Sunday) 10th June 1973 when he visited my home. Signed Eileen E. Horgan

Following identification, a post-mortem was carried out by Ireland's state pathologist, Professor Maurice Hickey, an austere, imposing man who was based at the Department of Forensic

Medicine at University College, Dublin. Professor Hickey's post-mortem report, which is included in the file, recounts in uncomfortable detail the examination of the body. It begins with an overview of the body as he saw it; build, height and appearance. The pathologist notes the absence of clothing and the rope used to tie both wrists. From here he goes into considerable detail explaining the nature of the brain injuries. There is little to be gained by reproducing the full extent of these observations, save to say that the injury was concentrated to the rear of the head, and that it was severe. Aside from this there were no other injuries apart from minor bruising on the shoulders and shins. Anyone examining this report would come to the merciful conclusion that the boy must not have suffered, that the blow was such that death would most likely have been instantaneous. Professor Hickey also confirms what others have stated: 'There was nothing in my examination to suggest that the deceased had suffered any form of sexual assault.' The report ends with the state pathologist's conclusion as to why the little boy's life had ended so prematurely: 'Death, in my opinion, was due to a fracture of the skull and contusion and laceration of the brain resulting from a severe blunt force injury or injuries on the back of the head.'

Almost exactly a month later, on Wednesday 11 July 1973, the Dublin city coroner, Dr Bartley Sheehan, presided over the inquest into the death of John Horgan. The file includes the names of the jury members, eight in total, all men. Dr Sheehan had only weeks earlier been appointed as Dublin County Coroner, having previously been established as a GP in the port town of Dun Laoghaire. He quickly grew into the job, winning friends and earning a great deal of respect along the way. He gave freely of his time to the families of those who had taken their own lives and had strong views on the increasing pressures placed on the '70s youth generation. He was never afraid to speak out on difficult issues, particularly concerning suicide, which at the time was seen by many as a taboo subject. On one occasion he spoke to a group at the launch of an art project relating to the coroner's court. One person who was there had the foresight to commit Dr Sheehan's thoughts to tape:

> All of you are going to be touched by a suicide sometime. Every one of you will know someone who took their own life. Each of you will, in the privacy of your own hearts, sometime wonder, 'If I'd said something different, if I'd said to that guy, "Would you like a cup of coffee?", if I'd said I'll talk a few more minutes instead of saying I've got to catch the bus, or I've got to be here, or there.' You will all come across that sometime: Would things have been different? So you're all going to be touched by a suicide and you'll all go away and wonder would you have made some difference, and the likelihood is that you might have. And I am saying that suicide, and these very sad deaths that we have to enquire into, are the unpleasant, shitty side of the human condition. They are the awful shittiness that exists in every culture. But the interesting thing about shit is that it is a fantastic fertiliser. And you know it's a really interesting thing when you talk to people like that, they say, 'Oh my God, it's terrible!' and they tell you a terrible story and you agree it's a terrible story, and you say, 'That's a terrible story, it's a heap of shit.' Now if you take the label off that and instead of a heap of shit, put on another label that says it's a heap of fertiliser . . .

Dr Bartley Sheehan was no stranger to challenging the status quo, though on that midweek morning in July 1973, his role was simply to establish the facts surrounding the death of the Horgan boy. At 11 a.m. precisely the proceedings began. The jury heard the Garda evidence, the testimony concerning the identification of the body and the detailed report by state pathologist, Professor Maurice Hickey. Then at some point, the proceedings were halted, the jury discharged, and the case adjourned – one can only assume that the intention was to reconvene once the criminal proceedings were complete.

Frustratingly the documents do not reveal precisely why the inquest was adjourned, why it was never reconvened and, crucially, why a death certificate was never issued. The authority that should have issued the certificate was the Office of the Dublin County Coroner. So perhaps today's coroner could shed some light on the case? After a series of phone calls and an exchange of emails, the coroner's office became increasingly baffled and perplexed. They had good reason to be anxious: when a person dies, there must be a death certificate. In every case, without exception. One reason is to prevent 'ghosting', a form of identity theft in which someone steals the identity of a dead person (the 'ghost'). Normally the person who steals this identity (the 'ghoster') is about the same age that the ghost would have been if still alive, so that any documents relating to the birth date of the ghost would look acceptable to someone scrutinising them. With no record of the boy's death, a Dublin man in his 40s – at the time of writing John Horgan would be 46 if he were still alive – could easily acquire an official copy of the boy's birth certificate, and then use it to gather other documentation in the name of John Joseph Horgan. At its most extreme, a fraudster could attempt to acquire a passport or even claim social security benefits.

The absence of a death certificate left the Dublin County Coroner with only one option: to re-open the inquest into the death of John Horgan, aged seven years, who died on 14 June 1973.

There was an atmosphere of euphoria among the staff and customers of the Maldron Hotel that May morning in 2011, a mood that had nothing at all to do with the proceedings in 'The Arena' meeting room, where the coroner's assistant was positioning chairs in preparation for the day's proceedings. One plush red chair with a gold cushion for the coroner was placed at the head of the room, there were tables where witnesses and families could sit, 12 seats for the jury, and a couple of dozen places at the rear for the press and public galleries. The excitement and euphoria, however, were directed towards an entirely separate event. Hours earlier, Air Force One had taken off from Dublin airport, following a hugely successful state visit to Ireland by United States President Barack Obama and First Lady Michelle Obama. The President had successfully traced his Irish roots, a distant link to the tiny rural village of Moneygall, from where his grandfather's grandfather had left for the New World, escaping the Irish famine of the 1840s. The trip was the main topic that morning and leading the discussion in the reception area was an American pensioner – a 'senior' as he preferred to be described – wearing a green T-shirt sporting the words 'There's no-one as Irish as Barack O'Bama.'

A few minutes before proceedings were due to begin, Dublin City Coroner Dr Kieran Geraghty sat alone in a small square anteroom next to the larger room where the inquest was about to start. Leafing through his caseload for the day, the middle-aged doctor, a bearded man with silver glasses, exuded an air of authority and intellect. As one of the country's most highly experienced coroners, Dr Geraghty has presided over some of the nation's most disturbing cases, from family fire tragedies to suspected infanticide. On the pink table cover placed in front of the coroner, that day's *Irish Independent* was open on the front page. Accompanying a photo of a beaming President Obama savouring a pint of Guinness at a pub in Moneygall with his recently discovered eighth cousin, 'Henry the Eighth', were banner headlines: three simple words spoken in the Irish language by the leader of the Free World: '*Is Féidir Linn*,' or, as the sentiment is more widely known, 'Yes We Can.'

Suddenly the door of the main room opened and everyone stood as the coroner took his place. Seated to Dr Geraghty's left was his assistant, whose job was to minute proceedings and to take oaths from sworn witnesses. Observing proceedings were a number of Garda police officers, two young men apparently awaiting a later inquest into the death of a friend, and a number of journalists all intrigued as to why an inquest was being held into the death of a little boy who had passed away 38 years earlier. There was no sign of Mr and Mrs Horgan. They were made aware that the inquest was taking place but had chosen to stay away. The coroner, Dr Geraghty, opened proceedings: 'I am here to open the inquest into the circumstances of the death of John Horgan, aged seven, who died on 14 June 1973.'

The first witness to be called identified himself as Detective Inspector Richard McDonnell from Lucan Garda Station. The coroner's office had notified DI McDonnell that no death certificate had been issued around the time of the Horgan boy's passing, and had requested that he investigate the circumstances of the case with a view to resolving this matter. Dr Geraghty added that a person had been charged in relation to the boy's death and that person was now living outside the jurisdiction. Given that the case had already been tried in a criminal court, he was not going to hear the case in full.

It was clear that the 2011 inquest was going to deal primarily with identification. To issue a death certificate, the coroner had ideally to hear from a witness who had seen the boy's body, a person who could recognise the boy's appearance, or at least have been with someone at the time who was able to recognise the body.

After being sworn in, Detective Inspector McDonnell confirmed that he had begun an investigation some three months earlier after receiving correspondence from the coroner. The plain-clothes police inspector confirmed that the Horgan boy was aged just seven at the time of his death, that he had been reported missing on 14 June 1973 and that later that night his body was found and identified. A person, only identified as a male, had been arrested, charged and sentenced. The detective inspector added that he had recently contacted the family of John Horgan who were absent from today's proceedings. He reported that they did not want to revisit this time in their lives and open old wounds. However he added that the boy's parents told him that their memories of their son were as strong today as they had ever been.

Next to be called was retired superintendent James Noonan. Despite having left the force some 14 years earlier, his memory was sharp and precise. On oath he confirmed that he was one of the investigators involved in the search for John Horgan that summer day in 1973. The journalists in the court sat to attention as Noonan said in a clear, steady voice that he had been present in the attic along with a priest, Reverend Father Richard Mulcahy, a family friend of the Horgans. He added that he and the priest had removed the body from the attic. Under questioning by the coroner, Noonan confirmed that the boy was known to Father Mulcahy.

This was a vital piece of evidence as it effectively identified the body here and now, in a coroner's court in 2011. Detective Sergeant Jim Noonan – as he was in 1973 – had seen the body in the company of Father Mulcahy, who knew the boy. Even though the priest was now dead, Noonan's memory of that encounter provided the missing jigsaw piece the coroner needed. The final piece of evidence was read to the court, a yellowing page, almost four decades old: the statement made by the late Father Mulcahy. The statement read,

> On the fourteenth of June 1973, I went to the home of my close friends, the Horgan family. Later in the company of Detective Sergeant James Noonan, I went to the attic of a neighbour's house where I saw the body of a young boy tied to the rafters. I identified this body as that of John Horgan. DS Noonan pointed out a communion chalice and three hosts which I removed. Later I helped DS Noonan remove the body from the attic.

At this point, the journalists present realised that what was being described was far from a tragic accident.

The coroner then announced that a post-mortem had been carried out by the late Professor Maurice Hickey, and briefly summarised the professor's findings. He added that he saw no reason to go into further details of the case and would only consider doing so if requested by the family or any other interested party.

Putting down his glasses he paused before extending his sincerest sympathy to the boy's parents. The coroner's conclusion was identical to that of Professor Hickey, that 'death, in my opinion, was due to a fracture of the skull and contusion and laceration of the brain resulting from a severe blunt force injury or injuries on the back of the head'. It was two weeks shy of thirty-eight years since young John Horgan had died in such bizarre and brutal circumstances. Now, at last, he had a death certificate to his name.

A record was broken that day: the adjourned inquest into the death of the Palmerstown boy, murdered 38 years previously, is understood to be the longest inquest in the history of the state. Previously that dubious honour was held by a case in County Leitrim, which was finally resolved in 2004. That too was a murder case; coincidentally, the state pathologist, Maurice Hickey, performed the autopsy, and the inquest was also re-opened because of a missing death certificate. It took 37 years to resolve the County Leitrim case. It is highly unusual and worth revisiting.

In re-opening that inquest, Sergeant John O'Donnell from Carrick-on-Shannon Garda Station explained that the original inquest was adjourned to allow for the completion of the criminal case against the assailant. But the inquest had then been forgotten somehow. The lapse only came to light when a death certificate was sought for the murdered man, Bernard McManus from Dromore, close to Ballinamore, in County Leitrim. His son, Vincent McManus, had wanted to sell some land, but he was stymied by an unexpected legal difficulty – he found that there was no death certificate in existence for his father because, as in the Horgan case, the original inquest into his father's death had never been completed.

The victim – Bernard McManus – was murdered near his home on Thursday, 13 April 1967. A local farm labourer was subsequently found guilty, but was judged to be insane and institutionalised behind the high walls of the Central Mental Hospital, Dundrum, a suburb of south Dublin.

Sergeant O'Donnell outlined the background of the case to the inquest. He said Mr McManus' death took place on his own farm as a result of receiving several fatal blows from a slash hook to the head. He was a 72-year-old retired farmer at the time of his death and was a widower living with his then 35-year-old son, Vincent. The assailant was 55-year-old James Gilchrist, who had been a farm labourer on the farm of Patrick Galligan, a near neighbour of the deceased.

For about six months prior to the incident, Mr Gilchrist was not on good terms with the McManuses, father and son. They had argued fiercely and often, though the fights had never become physical. On the day of the murder, Mr Gilchrist came home from Ballinamore, having had a few drinks of stout, and went to the nearby well where Bernard McManus happened to be. Words were exchanged. As a result of the altercation, Gilchrist walked to the house, took a slash hook and went after Bernard McManus. They met at a pigsty, and Gilchrist struck Mr McManus three times about the face and neck with the slash hook. The sound of the blows attracted the deceased's son, Vincent, who was only 60 yards away at the time. He witnessed the accused leaving the scene carrying the slash hook, after which he saw his father lying, covered in blood, at the entrance to the pigsty.

Bernard McManus died at the scene.

When police arrived to question James Gilchrist, he produced the slash hook, coated in fresh blood and, despite the warning not to speak before being cautioned, he said to them:

> I know what I done, I am not excited. I couldn't stick any more from that man. He put me to that pitch. Those people annoy you, especially when you are not in good form, and if you were far away you would be wondering what sort of man would do a thing like that.

191

That man got what he was looking for. He had me fairly persecuted since I came here. He didn't want me around the place.

Gilchrist was arrested and charged that same day. At his trial, the jury returned a verdict of guilty but insane. He remained in custody until his death.

At the re-opened inquest, Leitrim County Coroner, Dr Des Moran, said it was a sad death to have to revisit. He said death in this instance was caused by extensive injuries that were wielded with great vigour. He said Gilchrist must have had some sort of disturbance to do what he did. Dr Moran recommended to the jury that they record a verdict of death by unlawful killing.

Sergeant O'Donnell noted that it was probably the longest adjourned case in the history of the state and said he hoped it would finally bring closure to the case for the family of the deceased. He thanked the investigating Gardai from 1967 for attending the inquest, having travelled from Dublin and Galway.

No one present would have imagined that just seven years later an even longer adjourned inquest would be re-opened, to bring closure to the John Horgan case once and for all.

# EIGHT

# Forgive Us Those who Trespass Against Us

If the murders of children are mercifully rare, the murders of children by other children are even more infrequent. On the tragic occasions where a child's life is taken, the event's rarity invariably makes the story headline news. Assuming that a suspect is apprehended and charged, the subsequent trial affords an opportunity for the detail of the murder to be read into open court, effectively putting the minutiae of the killing into the public domain. The inquisitive devour the papers, follow the broadcast news and, to satisfy their own curiosity, discover 'the five Ws' of murder: who, why, what, where and when? However, the true identity of the killer of little John Horgan is largely unknown to Irish people, due principally to one factor: Lorcan Bale's age.

The murder happened when Lorcan Bale was aged sixteen years and two months; by the time his trial took place he was sixteen years and seven months. Under Irish law juveniles age twelve and over are considered old enough to be prosecuted. Had the crime happened in another country, such as Belgium, the process may have been different. The UN Convention on the Rights of the Child sets out, under Article 40, that states should establish 'a minimum age below which children shall be presumed not to have the capacity to infringe the penal law'. While this is a fine sentiment, the Convention offers no guidance on what this age should be; countries are left to decide it for themselves. The inconsistencies between international jurisdictions are profound. The UNICEF Committee on the Rights of the Child reports that in India, Singapore and Thailand children reach the age of criminal responsibility at just seven, as compared to age eighteen in Belgium and Argentina. England, Wales, Northern Ireland, Australia and Switzerland may try children for criminal acts once they are ten, whereas Ireland shares the age of twelve with Scotland, Japan and Israel.

Because he was over the age of twelve, the Irish legal system deemed that Lorcan Bale had reached the age of criminal responsibility. He could be tried. However he was not an adult and as a juvenile – the term used in many international jurisdictions to describe a person under 18 – the legal system offered him some protection. Most valuable, from Lorcan Bale's point of view, is that Irish law prevents journalists from naming a juvenile facing criminal charges.

Back in 1973, as word began to spread among the press that here was a unique murder trial, the killing of a child by a child, reporters were eagerly anticipating the courtroom drama. Soon rumours began to emerge that the murder had occult overtones, and that the body of the victim had been found 'crucified' in a neighbour's attic. The truth behind these rumours was expected to emerge at the trial, and while journalists knew that the perpetrator could not be named in their daily dispatches, the detail of the case was so sensational it would be guaranteed headline news. Press interest was not confined to Ireland. Reporters converged on Dublin's Central Criminal Court from many leading English newspapers; some even arrived from further afield, including reporters from New York, Montreal and Los Angeles. On the morning of the trial they were all crammed into the press bench of the courtroom, eagerly awaiting what they hoped would be the most sensational trial of the modern Irish state.

They were to be disappointed. The accused, Lorcan Bale, uttered only one word: 'Guilty.' With that, the trial was effectively over. The police witnesses all breathed a sigh of relief: they would be spared the lengthy process of giving evidence and showing exhibits. The jury was discharged and sentence was passed. The headline-hungry journalists, some of whom had travelled thousands of miles, were left with nothing. The following day, 28 November 1973, the *Irish Times* published a small report, buried on page seven under the headline, 'Youth gets Life Sentence':

> A sentence of penal servitude for life was imposed in the Central Criminal Court in Dublin yesterday on a sixteen-year-old youth who pleaded guilty to the murder of John Horgan of 6 Hollyville, Lucan Road, Palmerstown on June fourteenth last.
>
> In passing sentence, Mr Justice Kenny recommended that the youth should serve the sentence in St Patrick's Institution until he reaches the age of twenty one, when he would be transferred to another prison. Mr Gerard Clarke, Senior Counsel for the Attorney General said the accused boy had not yet reached his seventeenth birthday. Inquiries into the murder were conducted, particularly by Garda Detective Inspector Reynolds, and eventually a full statement was made by the accused and all the facts were made clear.

That was it. No name, no detail, just the barest of bare minimums. The assembled reporters folded their notebooks and left empty handed. They knew when they were beaten.

In contrast to the story of John Horgan's death, there have been isolated cases of murdered children in Ireland where the press and news-hungry readers have had a field day. It is hardly worth blaming journalists for writing about murder – the public appetite for crime is huge, and when the crime is murder and there is a child involved, there is no apparent limit to the reader's interest.

While the public may be interested, whether such voraciousness or the coverage it generates is itself in the public interest is another debate for another day.

In the history of the modern Irish state, Lorcan Bale, as a child killer, is a member of a tiny group of people: the number of children murdered in the country has been mercifully low. When such killings do occur (it can be decades between one case and the next), the shock is profound. There was widespread media coverage of the tragic death in January 2005 of 11-year-old Cork boy Robert Holohan, killed by a 20-year-old neighbour. The accused, Wayne O'Donoghue, admitted killing the boy next door, stating that the death was an accident following a row that had erupted when Robert threw stones at his car. Acquitted of murder, O'Donoghue served three years of a four-year sentence for manslaughter. That death prompted journalists to dust down the archives of other murders over the past four decades. In April 1970, three years before the death of John Horgan, ten-year-old Bernadette Connolly was abducted near her home in Sligo. Her body was found four months later and an autopsy revealed that the youngster had been sexually assaulted and strangled. Her killer was never caught. Just over a year later, in July 1971, an eight-year-old boy, Vincent Blackwell, from Finglas, North Dublin, was found dead on wasteland about a mile from his home. Little Vincent's body was found by a teenage boy who was playing in the area at the time along with scores of other children. The case was barely reported on at the time, but one quote from the boy who found the child's remains revealed: 'Three girls were playing "chasing" and they called me over. They said there was something in the bushes. I looked and I found a body.' The young witness added, 'I went and told the Guards.' It emerged that young Vincent had been strangled by a boy who lived close to the Blackwells' home. The killer was just 15 when he took young Vincent's life. Some months later, at Dublin's Central Criminal Court, the teenager was convicted of manslaughter and instructed to seek mental health treatment.

Later, in 1977, in Donegal, six-year-old Mary Boyle mysteriously disappeared. The child's body was never recovered and the case remains unsolved.

Another unexplained disappearance, and perhaps the case with the highest profile in recent years, was that of Philip Cairns, the Dublin teenager who vanished on his way back to school after lunch in October 1986. Days later his schoolbag was found in an alleyway near his home in the south Dublin suburb of Rathfarnham. His body was never found and the schoolboy remains officially 'missing'. There has been widespread speculation about what happened in the Cairns case, but no line of enquiry has proven firm enough to warrant an arrest and conviction.

The disappearance of Philip Cairns prompted some newspaper reports to assert that Robert Holohan, Bernadette Connolly and – assuming they too have perished – Philip Cairns and Mary Boyle were the only four children abducted and murdered in the history of the Irish state. No mention whatsoever was made of John Horgan, despite the extraordinary circumstances of his death. His killing had, quite simply, fallen off the radar.

But there was another child murder case that has also been largely forgotten – one that bears similarities to the death of the Horgan boy. That is the killing of five-year-old Tommy Powell, who lived in Cuffe Street in Dublin's inner city, and who disappeared on 20 June 1961 after he had left his house to visit his aunt nearby. While the deaths of Tommy Powell and John Horgan are unconnected, there was a theory – one that remains unproven – that he too may have been killed by another child. Two local teenagers from Ross Road, Christopher Ellis and Michael Gavin, found his fully clothed body the next day in a graveyard on Liberty Lane, just a few hundred yards from his home. The old graveyard – which is now a small park – was often used by local children as a play area.

A few yards away from the spot where the body was found were two large, bloodstained rocks. It was a truly grisly scene: there were several bloodstains on the walls and grass, and the body had extensive head injuries. Little Tommy had, it seemed, been battered to death. His remains were removed to the city morgue in Dublin's Store Street, where the state pathologist, Dr Maurice Hickey – the same man who years later would examine the body of John Horgan – carried out a post-mortem. The victim's sixth birthday had been just three weeks away. By all accounts Tommy came from a good family. He had a two-year-old younger brother, James, and, according to his parents, he was not in the habit of wandering far from home. At the time it would not have been unusual for small children to be in the graveyard, which was viewed as a safe communal play area.

The police inquiry focused initially on the notion that Tommy was killed in a hit-and-run accident, speculating that a driver had struck the boy, panicked, and carried the body to the graveyard before driving off. Another line of inquiry suggested that he may have climbed onto the wall of the graveyard and fallen, fatally injuring his head. This scenario was given some credence days later when a photographer from the *Irish Press*, Seán Larkin, fell and broke both his arms while taking photographs of the crime scene after the body had been found. One theory was that the boy's body had been thrown over the wall by an older child after Tommy was accidently killed by another child in play. But could children so calmly dispose of a body and then remain cool when under police questioning? Could they guard such a terrible secret for so long? Children being children, surely one of them would let the truth slip out eventually?

Painstaking house-to-house inquiries were carried out in the area where Tommy Powell had last been seen, and thousands of questionnaires were distributed, returned and analysed. Police believed that someone, somewhere, could unlock this mystery: it was inconceivable, they surmised, that absolutely nobody had seen anything odd. Ten days later, Gardai were still making daily appeals for people to step forward with information, 'however insignificant it may appear'. They also said, 'We believe that there are others who can assist and are hesitant to come forward.'

Could the missing link be the man who had been removed to Grangegorman Mental Hospital on the night Tommy was murdered following a scene in O'Connell Street, in which he appeared disoriented, incoherent and unable to remember his name? He was questioned by the police, but turned out to have a cast-iron alibi, so was ruled out as a suspect. Also investigated was the sighting of a boy with a young-looking man on Burgh Quay late on the Tuesday night, but he was also ruled out as a suspect. So too was a man reported to be acting strangely in a Dublin pub on the same night. He was interviewed at Kevin Street station but, again, a connection with the murder was not established.

Most intriguingly, and perhaps most sickeningly, an anonymous letter was sent to the Gardaí in which the author suggested he or she could help with solving the murder. The letter was initialled 'DC' and was handed in to Kevin Street station. The letter asked the Gardaí to insert a notice in newspapers saying 'OK DC' if they wanted to make further contact. They duly did this, but there was no response.

By the end of the first week in July it was reported that the Gardaí were cooperating with police in England in order to interview a number of people who left the Cuffe Street district after the murder. They also visited all factories and schools in the vicinity of Cuffe Street in an effort to trace Tommy's last movements. Up to the second week in July the hunt was intensified and Gardaí spent a full day interviewing about 30 boys from the area, after which they were convinced that the murderer had been seen by several of them, and that the killer was still in the area. But their frustration, and the agony of his family, continued. There were no new developments, which must have been particularly perplexing given the belief that the murderer was still near by. The Gardaí also informed the media that 'in spite of numerous appeals by the police, very little assistance has been given to them by the public'. Why, in Dublin over a half-century ago, was this the case? Who handed in the letter to Kevin Street station, who wrote it, and why? Are there people still alive who know who killed Tommy Powell? It is a tragic case, one where the file remains open.

Three decades after the murder of Tommy Powell, 23-year-old Lorcan Bale was a free man. The majority of his former schoolmates in Coláiste Mhuire had completed their tertiary education and were beginning to make their mark on the world. Most of them were enjoying conventional, successful lives, some in Ireland, others abroad. The freed felon, for his part, had gained an education behind bars, having both passed his Leaving Certificate – the final secondary school exams – and completed a university degree course. Yet the first 23 years of Bale's life had been anything but conventional: a sickly child who had endured a number of confinements in hospital, his schooling disrupted by illness; a former altar boy whose lips had tasted theft; a torturer of animals; a teenager with a growing interest in the occult; the constructor of an elaborate satanic shrine in the attic of his family's home; the murderer of an innocent young boy. This heinous act brought the teenager into the court system: he spent five months as a remand prisoner before being convicted for murder and beginning a life sentence. Initially confined to a borstal, St Patrick's Institution, until being transferred to an adult prison at the age of 21, he was a model, if unconventional, prisoner. Now seven-and-a-half years after killing the Horgan boy, Lorcan Bale was free to make his way in the world, to chase his ambitions, to be the person that he believed he should always have been.

In the months after his release, he spent much of his time at the Bale house in Glasnevin, north Dublin, where the entire family had hurriedly moved in the weeks following the murder. That he was welcomed back into the family home does not come as a great surprise, the bonds of family being the closest ties of all. However, eyebrows were raised by some people in Dublin who were familiar with the case, on hearing that the child killer was once again walking the city's streets.

One former prisoner who befriended Bale while behind bars

recalled, 'I saw him across the dance floor in The Pink Elephant' – one of Dublin's racier '80s nightclubs. 'Our eyes met and he turned away immediately. I never saw him again.' There were all kinds of rumours floating around Dublin, a city where conversation is the national sport, a town where secrets are rarely kept for long. Some claimed to have seen Bale working in a bar; others said he was playing in a band. Another rumour circulated stating that he had used connections to secure a job in Ireland's civil service. The more fanciful said he had met a nun, fallen in love and had asked her to marry him. A more reliable report had him visiting Hollyville, walking along the road where he had once lived. Now in his 20s, Bale looked dishevelled and gaunt; he was dressed in army fatigues with long hair and a beard. He struck up a conversation with an elderly resident enquiring who was still living in the area. Apart from this incident, he appears to have assiduously avoided his old friends from Palmerstown and Coláiste Mhuire. It was as if he had taken a clear and conscious decision to put his past behind him and to move forward independently.

After my eight-month investigation into the murder of the little Horgan boy – a process that involved interviewing dozens of people, assembling facts and pouring over many lost documents – there remained one silent voice. We still don't know what Lorcan Bale was thinking and feeling as he sat in that attic staring at a dead child.

If you were to meet Lorcan Bale on the street, what are the unanswered questions that only he can answer? The biggest of all has to be: 'Why?' What drove him to take the life of his defenceless young neighbour? Did he really believe that he needed to kill a child in a weird, satanic black mass? And what of his influences? Were other adults encouraging him on a path that would eventually lead to murder? And finally, today, as an adult, how does he rationalise the enormity of his actions? How has he changed? Is he filled with regret? Does he think every day of the Horgan family, the good people that they are, and the indescribable pain he caused when he snatched away their only son?

As an author, I cannot answer these questions. Neither can any of the witnesses I have interviewed for this book. There is only one person who can unlock these secrets, one man who jealously guards these almost forgotten facts. For several days, I pondered a dilemma. I knew his name, I knew his date of birth: Lorcan Bale had by now to be in his 50s, that is, assuming he were still alive. He had served his time, albeit just seven years; and he could well now have a family of his own who may know nothing of his past. It was important to seek answers but equally important to be fair. After weighing up all the facts, the decision I took was to find him, observe and, in due course, approach. But – and it is a big 'but' – at no stage would I reveal in this book the job that he does, where he works, his address or even the country where he lives. This was in part recognition of his young age at the time of the offence, in part an acknowledgement of the fact that he had paid his debt to society, but more importantly it was a protection of those close to him today. He could be married, perhaps have children of his own – all entirely innocent parties, individuals who should not be identified in this book or indeed in any other publication. As long as there was no evidence that he was a continued danger to the public, then I resolved not to reveal his whereabouts.

Ireland is a small country, with a population of just four-and-a-half million. A public records search revealed no death certificate in Bale's name, so the odds were good that he was still alive, though of course he might have died abroad. Further detailed enquiries also drew a blank, indicating with near certainty that he was not living within the jurisdiction of the Republic of Ireland. The United States and Australia are highly popular destinations for Irish people willing to start a new life abroad: both English-speaking, both dynamic economies where an Irish accent is not quite a passport to employment, but not far off. However a check with the American immigration department revealed that anyone who has ever been arrested – even if totally innocent – or convicted of any offence – except very minor motoring offences – is ineligible to enter the USA under the visa waiver programme. A convicted felon would have to formally apply for an entry visa; the chances of a child murderer's application being successful are just above nil. The Australian authorities were of a similar mind. They said that for a normal visitor visa, 'You must not have any criminal convictions for which the sentence is a total period of 12 months duration or more, at the time of travel to, and entry into, Australia.'

With Ireland, America and Australia ruled out, logically he must surely be residing within the European Union, where an EU passport allows the bearer to live and work largely without hindrance. After detailed enquiries in several of the member states, one possible lead pointed to an ornate church in a European capital where a person called 'Lorcan Bale' had been working as a church warden. With a potential location established, the only thing to do was visit, seek out the church and see if the man could be found.

Touching down early on a Sunday morning, I arrived at the red brick church just as the congregation were assembling for morning prayers. This was a family occasion in an affluent part of town; of the 30 or so in the congregation, almost half were children. I sat in the back row and watched the people arriving intently. If Lorcan Bale was among their number, his presence was not at all obvious. One man looked to be about the right age, but when he stood to sing, it was clear he was taller than Bale. The killer's height – 5 ft 6 in – was not something he could hide. Somewhat disheartened by what appeared to be another cold lead, I joined the congregation afterwards to chat about the church, the surroundings and the issues that mattered to them. Quite accidentally, when preparing to leave this serene place of worship, something caught my eye. On the wall just inside the wooden door was a mahogany plaque listing the names of donors to a 2004 church restoration fund. Etched in gold lettering beneath the 11 generous benefactors was the name of a church official: Lorcan Bale. With such an unusual name, this had to be him. But why was a once self-confessed satanist now helping out in a Christian church? Had he undergone some form of conversion? Was this an epiphany driven by guilt and remorse? The list of questions was growing ever longer.

Having established which town he worked in, a search of electoral records there revealed that until 2008 he had lived near a hospital in the city. A second search produced what appeared to be a current address, a place to call home in a pleasant part of the town, a suburb with all the amenities for modern life close at hand.

The tools of an investigative journalist are not those that the casual observer would normally expect. A camera with a long lens is essential, a car with mirrored windows to allow photography without suspicion comes a close second, but no self-respecting stakeout is complete without a flask of strong coffee, a punnet of good fresh fruit and a pee bottle. Observation always takes twice as long as planned, but is an essential part of the job. Stakeouts and snooping are close relations. Neither is particularly tasteful, but the stakeout is a crucial strategy in the work of a journalist. Most reporters shun the confrontational paparazzi approach: the most effective method is to quietly blend in, to ask casual questions, to obey traffic laws, not to trespass on private property and definitely never to rummage through a person's bins.

Early on that cool morning, the hire car – carefully selected for its darkened windows – was parked in prime position with a clear view of the address, a modern apartment block, red brick, of '90s construction. Three large recycling bins for communal use were positioned next to the entrance to an underground car park for the benefit of the building's hundred or so residents. This was a very typical suburb of a European city: buses ferried early commuters to work, a few hardy cyclists braved the traffic, joggers were in the final stage of training for a marathon that would take place the following weekend, and the occasional pensioner could be seen walking with their dog. White cherry blossom trees with bird tables built into their branches provided refuge for a pair of grey squirrels scavenging from the recycling bins. It was a very ordinary place, with one exception: directly opposite the front door of the apartment block – barely 50 yards away – was the unmistakeable signage of a primary school. Many of the apartment balconies overlooked the school playground; surely this could not be a place that a convicted child murderer would call home?

The stakeout proved to be a worthwhile exercise. A later analysis of the photographs taken while observing the comings and goings of the block revealed more than expected. The apartment block was its own mini Tower of Babel, one that housed a melting pot of nationalities: Afro-Caribbean, Indian, Chinese, Muslim women with ornate headscarves, several tanned Mediterranean types, yet very few pale Caucasian men. However, one man looked a likely match: small, tightly shaven grey hair, early 50s with a few days beard growth, 80s-style gold-rimmed shades, a squat man with a distinct middle-aged paunch. The trail pointed to this man, but only through speaking to him could the hunch be ultimately confirmed.

The following weekend I returned to the apartment block, arriving on a bright spring morning. Little had changed from the previous week: the bins were in exactly the same spot, as were the squirrels; there was the same hustle and bustle with cars pulling up outside, many picking up youngsters involved in Saturday morning sports. Inside, a middle-aged man was relaxing, another week's work having been completed. He had no way of knowing that he was about to receive a visitor concerned with his distant past, one with news of events that most in his world were either unaware of or had largely forgotten. At the entrance, I considered again the moral and practical questions that had been floating through my mind over the previous weeks. How would he react to the knock at his door? I had already decided not to enter the building and meet inside his own apartment, not due to fears for my personal safety, but because there was no way of knowing who else would be present, perhaps friends or loved ones who had no knowledge of Bale's past. The ideal place to meet was on neutral territory, outside the apartment block, ideally on a bench at the nearby park.

At the main entrance was a video intercom of the type where the caller keys in the apartment number, and the resident can look at the visitor's face captured on camera below before deciding whether to respond. After punching in the number, and standing in clear camera view, I waited. A man's voice with a soft but unmistakeable Irish accent answered.

'Is that Lorcan?' I asked.

There was a hesitation before the man replied. 'Yes.'

Stepping forward to the intercom, I spoke slowly and clearly to avoid any misunderstanding.

'Lorcan, we haven't met before. My name is David Malone. I'm an author and television producer, though today I'm speaking to you only as an author. I have come from Ireland to speak with you about a family matter. Would you mind if we met outside? I'll wait for you here.' There was a pause and then the intercom crackled into life.

'Give me a few minutes.' Ten minutes later a portly middle-aged man bounded through the glass doors. 'Sorry,' he said, 'I was in the bathroom.'

We shook hands, looked at each other – he clearly unsure where this conversation was headed. This was Lorcan Bale, the murderer of little John Horgan, standing casually outside his home, his pale face bathed in early spring sunshine. Small and stocky, he was absolutely unrecognisable from the photograph of the exam student published in the newspaper over 30 years ago. The youngster's gaunt features had been replaced by the physique of a man who was living a sedentary, white-collar lifestyle. The teenager's thick, long, black hair was now a thinning, tightly cut, grey covering. That morning, being a day off work, he was casually dressed in a blue-and-white-checked shirt, loosely fitting dark trousers and light trainers.

After repeating the introductions made over the intercom, I spoke in a low voice, not wanting to appear in any way threatening. The news Bale was about to hear would inevitably come as a shock to him and there was no reason to antagonise him further by speaking loudly or with aggression. Looking at him squarely in the eyes, I told him I was writing a book that would detail the events that took place in Palmerstown in 1973. After a pause to give him time to digest the information, I asked if he understood what I was saying. He swallowed, then nodded, his already pale face having turned white, a transformation his greying beard struggled to hide. We shifted over to a low wall beside the driveway to leave the path clear for two loud young Asian boys approaching on skateboards.

Having earlier considered at length what his response might be – and discounted a violent reaction, one that would have been completely out of character for the adult Lorcan Bale – there were three options available to him: opening up and telling all, walking away while refusing to comment or stalling to buy time.

'I need to talk to some people before I can talk to you about this matter,' said Bale eventually, his voice shaking slightly. Expecting as much, I explained in some detail why he had received a knock on his door that morning. Firstly he should be made aware that a book about an important part of his life would be published in the months ahead; secondly to inform him of the now reconvened inquest into the death of John Horgan. I deliberately studied Bale's eyes at the moment when for the first time I spoke the name of the boy whose life he had stolen, wondering what telltale signs his face would give away. Would he wince? Or shake his head? Or show signs of irritation? But disappointingly there was absolutely nothing, his expression frozen like a rabbit caught in headlights. The middle-aged man just uttered a few words of acknowledgement to say he understood what was being said. We spoke in more general terms for ten more minutes, perhaps for a little longer, he leaning against the wall that supported the apartment entrance. In that time, what came across most was his ordinariness. There was not even the slightest hint of the reckless, wayward teenager who had stolen bikes, money and Communion silverware all those years ago. Neither were there any detectable signs of anything sinister: he just looked and behaved like a regular, middle-aged bloke with a normal nine-to-five routine. If you were asked to pick him out of an identity parade as the person who had killed a seven-year-old in part of a bizarre satanic ritual, your eyes would skip past him without a pause.

Our conversation broadened. He revealed that he remained in touch with his brother and sisters, adding, 'The family is very solid.' I told him that I did not want this book to overly affect his current life, that I had not and would not approach his siblings, that I would not reveal his whereabouts, not least because it was now clear that he had never committed a criminal offence since that June day in 1973. Proposing that in the coming weeks we could meet in Dublin, he smiled and said that he would be in the Irish capital the following month – a knowing smile that suggested to me he might be referring to the meeting with justice ministry officials that all prisoners released on licence must undergo every year. We talked briefly about Coláiste Mhuire and, thinking about Lorcan Conroy, who had expressed a desire to reunite with his former schoolmate after all these years, I told him that one of his former classmates would perhaps like to meet once again. 'Oh Lord,' he mumbled, rolling his eyes, adding, 'maybe not.' Bale laughed nervously, moved towards the door saying, 'As you will appreciate, I'll need to talk to a few people and get advice about this.'

Leaving a card with my contact details, I shook his hand. Bale's was a firm, solid handshake, yet for the few seconds that our hands were interlocked, I was deeply conscious that this was the very same palm that had with such brute force snuffed out an innocent child's life. Walking away, and considering all that was said, the meeting had gone as well as could be expected.

After several days without any contact from Bale, a fear, which had been present throughout my search for his present whereabouts, began to grow. How would having to revisit the events of 1973 affect his mental health? As every day went by without a response, my anxiety increased. I had discovered where he worked and the nature of his job, a secure position in an office environment. However, given the fact that my enquiry had nothing whatsoever to do with his job, I resisted calling or emailing him at his workplace. Instead, I wrote a follow-up letter.

Dear Lorcan,

I hope you are keeping well.

I didn't want to contact you at your work and, being too far away to ring your doorbell again, thought it best to drop you this note.

As I explained when we met at the weekend, I am a writer and TV producer, currently writing a non-fiction book about the events in Palmerstown in 1973. Obviously as your story is very much at the centre of those events, it is essential that I keep you properly informed. While I am sure that you would much rather that this topic were not revisited, the new inquest scheduled for next month will inevitably put some facts into the public domain.

I would like to sit down with you, ideally within the next couple of weeks. At that meeting, I hope we can be open and frank with each other. For my part, I will tell you in detail the content of the book, also when and where it will be published. In addition, I will brief you on the inquest date, which I do not believe will impact upon you, except as I explained to potentially create some press interest. You have my assurance that I will work with you to ensure that the publication of the book will not overly impact on the life that you presently lead. By this, I mean avoiding publishing certain information, particularly concerning where you live and work.

My arrival on your doorstep must surely have come as a shock to you. While outwardly you appeared calm, it must have been difficult to revisit with a relative stranger the events of over thirty years ago. You may remember Dr Brian McCaffrey, who counselled you while on remand; I approached him some weeks ago to interview him about his work. Obviously he could not talk about your specific case due to patient confidentiality, but when I told him that I was going to visit you, he said that if you wanted to talk to a sympathetic ear, in absolute confidence, to a person who is familiar with your case, he would happily talk to you. His number is [number redacted].

To give you something more to consider, whenever we meet, I am not intending to dwell upon the tragic events of 14th June 1973. Instead, I will press you on how you got there. While all the evidence states that you acted alone, I believe it likely that you were influenced by others. You disappeared for four days in December 1972, perhaps to meet adults in County Meath . . .

Another area I would like to discuss is your relationship with your late father, also how the events have impacted upon your adult life. I believe that you have a definite religious faith and would like to develop this theme with you.

Lorcan, my contact details are below. I look forward to talking with you soon.

With best regards.

Yours sincerely,

David Malone

After several more days, and still with no reply, I relented and sent a short email to his work, avoiding mention of the subject under discussion in case a work colleague should read the message.

----- Original Message -----
From: David Malone
To: Lorcan Bale
Sent: 14:19 hrs
Subject: Letter
Dear Lorcan,
I hope you are keeping well.
A quick note to ask if you received my letter? I sent it last week, but it could have been delayed by the holiday post. If it hasn't yet landed, I can email it to you, but probably better to a personal email account.
Best for now,
David Malone

Less than 20 minutes later, there was a reply.

----- Original Message -----
From: Lorcan Bale
To: David Malone
Sent: 14:36 hrs
Subject: RE: Letter
Dear David,
I received and read it last night. The contents are under consideration.
I shall send you an email address and telephone number as a more appropriate contact as you suggested. This should happen on Friday.
My wife and I are going away for the weekend (without my laptop) to return Monday night.
Regards,
Lorcan

Short and very much to the point, the mail was in its own way quite revealing. Terse, exceedingly formal, with a bare minimum of politeness, it suggested that he was far from happy – a hardly unexpected reaction. The reference to sending his personal contact details on Friday said quite clearly that he will email, but he is not at all interested in a response, a dialogue.

And then there is the weekend away with his wife. The revelation that he is married is eye-opening. He is surely confiding in her at this moment. At best, she is understanding and supportive, giving him advice on how to deal with his past being revisited after all these years. At worst, she is unaware that the man with whom she shared her wedding vows is a convicted satanic child killer. If that is the position, Lorcan Bale is truly in a very lonely place.

Still. At least he is OK.

True to his word, the following Friday another email message arrived:

----- Original Message -----
From: Mr L Bale
To: David Malone
Sent: 15:30 hrs
Subject: 1973
Dear David,

As promised, I am providing you with a personal email address and my mobile phone number as an alternative to you contacting me at my present place of work.

The number is [number redacted].

I shall not be contactable until Monday as we are going away for the weekend. You are welcome to test the email or the phone until this evening.

The present position is that I am not at liberty to contact you, even if I so wished, but I shall be having a meeting with a person from the Department of Justice in Dublin on Wednesday and my view will be that a

line of communication should be kept open.
Regards,
Lorcan

A further exchange saw us agreeing to sit tight until after the meeting between Bale and officials from the Irish justice ministry. The most likely outcome of that meeting and of others, including talks with family members, was that he would be advised to 'plead the fifth', that is, to refuse to be interviewed on the grounds that he might have more to lose than to gain.

A few days after the Dublin meeting, I called him on the mobile number he had supplied. Having exchanged text messages earlier that day, he was expecting the call.

To refer to the call as a 'conversation' would be stretching the word to its absolute limits. Bale sounded very nervous, there were long silent pauses and the few words he spoke were chosen with great care. It was as if he had received professional advice to say as little as possible, to commit to nothing but at the same time to maintain a dialogue. Nothing was agreed except that we would keep in touch.

The following Monday night, shortly after midnight, he wrote:

----- Original Message -----
From: Mr L Bale
To: David Malone
Sent: 00:47 hrs
Subject: no subject
David,
I hope that you understand that I must decline. I do not wish to discuss anything with you and I have no intention of doing so.
Regards,
Lorcan.

It was a disappointing but not an unexpected response; if anything the main surprise was the length of time it took for him to reach this conclusion.

Ex-prisoners, in whatever country they live, find it notoriously difficult to re-integrate into society; former prisoners with a murder conviction even more so. Yet to Lorcan Bale's credit he has successfully rebuilt his life: he has a wife, a home, a tertiary-level qualification, a fulfilling and secure job. It is understood that he never re-offended and therefore poses no danger to the public at large. Employment practices in his new country are such that whenever he applies for a job, he is under an obligation to declare whether he has any criminal convictions. So it is fair to assume that his employer is aware of his background but must deem it irrelevant to his job because the offence happened so long ago and because he has integrated successfully into society. His work is administrative and does not involve contact with children, indeed it would be highly unlikely that he would ever be permitted to work with children or vulnerable people.

If Lorcan Bale were unwilling to talk about life after prison, one person who could give an honest sense of what it must be like for him is Bobby Cummines, a colourful Londoner who, like Bale, began his criminal life at the tender age of 16. Cummines' first serious conviction as a teenager was for possession of a firearm, securing him the dubious honour of being one of the youngest people in the UK convicted of carrying a sawn-off shotgun. Later he became a notorious gangland leader and was convicted of a number of serious offences, including manslaughter and bank robbery. At the height of his notoriety, he was labelled as one of 'Britain's Most Wanted' and, when eventually captured, was sentenced to 20 years behind bars. With remission, Bobby Cummines was released after 13 years, despite being a disruptive prisoner involved in prison riots and spending time in solitary confinement. In prison he was somebody, but on release nobody wanted to know.

When I came out, I was really affected by my record. At first

I told the truth, but as soon as that happened the door was shut on me. So I thought to myself: 'OK, there's only one way to do it. Don't declare it.' So I didn't. Which caused another problem because then I had to make up a whole history of where I'd been for the last 12 years.

Then I got little bits of jobs, cash in hand, those sorts of things. People saw I was good and wasn't offending, so they gave me more. I did a lot of voluntary work with ex-offenders and I got the volunteer of the year award from the Society of Voluntary Associates.

Eventually I got a full-time job and from then on I stayed in the workplace. I was made redundant but didn't go back to crime. I just got another job. I'm well on my way now. It was mostly done with support from my now ex-wife and friends I met working. When a job came up, they'd say: 'Bob's good. He can do that.' They trusted me, and I moved on.

Today Bobby Cummines is chief executive of Unlock, an association of ex-offenders, and is a government advisor on the rehabilitation of former prisoners. He considered Lorcan Bale's case and offered some interesting insights into the problems he may have faced upon release. Aside from obvious difficulties finding a job, he may have had problems with insurance. The experience of Bobby Cummines is that most insurance companies will not issue cover for home policies to former prisoners, deeming them to be an excessive risk. Failure to declare a previous conviction can render an insurance policy invalid. Similarly some landlords may be unwilling to rent out a room to a former offender.

Another very practical problem faced by ex-prisoners is a lack of access to banking facilities. Without a bank account, employers are often reluctant to give a person a job.

The final area of advice proffered by Bobby Cummines concerned relationships. A person with a serious conviction, particularly anything that involves violence against children, needs to be extremely careful about who they tell. 'The only way to deal with this is to act on a need-to-know basis,' observed Cummines. There comes a point in a relationship when the former offender must tell the truth to their partner, even if that risks losing forever the person they love. But, said Cummines, 'It's important to recognise that people can change, that a person today may not be the same person they were many years ago.' While a criminal record is not an automatic bar to adoption of children, a person of Lorcan Bale's background would be highly unlikely to be approved for adopting a child, in whatever jurisdiction he lives.

We all carry secrets, most mercifully trivial. But how heavy must the burden be of carrying the secret of having spent many years in prison – of being a lifer who committed that most heinous of crimes, the premeditated murder of a child? The easiest way to counter this weight is to be completely open, for everyone to know your background, metaphorically wearing a T-shirt with the words 'Child Killer' emblazoned on the chest. However, in the real world this is clearly impractical, so some form of secrecy is essential. It would have been valuable to ask Lorcan Bale how he manages the truth of his past – who among his friends and family is aware of his background, and who is not. For in answering that question, one reveals that there is a thin line of deception, with a few trusted people embracing the secret but with the rest of society excluded. Managing the secret is just one part of dealing with the yoke of being a convicted murderer.

The restrictions on travel, home insurance and personal finance issues as put forward by Barry Cummines may be other factors. But only the killer himself can state the weight of the emotional baggage that he carries. At one end of the scale is the cold-hearted killer, the person with no regard for his victim or the consequences of what he has done. This person would have put the crime to one side, rationalised to himself that all of this was in the past and life for him must continue. At the other extreme is the person whose every waking moment is filled with regret, an all-consuming guilt that recognises the enormity of the crime. The most likely place for Lorcan Bale – or indeed any murderer – is somewhere in the middle. Shame and regret can be positive emotions if they are countered by practical moves to reform and atone.

Perhaps Bale learned from the experience of others, saw the predicament of other ex-prisoners, rationalised, then said to himself, 'I'm not following his path . . .' At the time of writing, a murder case in India is receiving wide press attention in the sub-continent, as much for the demeanour of the killer as for the murder itself. Just a day after he used a khukuri – a type of Indian machete used by Ghurkha soldiers – to murder Khusboo Kumari, supposedly the love of his life, Bijendra Prasad believes he must now atone.

'Let the court hang me or award me life imprisonment. I am not worried,' declared the girl's murderer. 'I have committed a huge mistake and do not want to save myself at any cost. I will neither appoint any lawyer nor file any bail application in court. I just want to live and die in jail,' he told reporters while waiting in a van with six armed policemen keeping watch.

An exchange between this self-confessed killer, wracked with guilt, and a crowd of waiting journalists is typical of a person at the most regretful extreme of the scale:

Reporter: 'Why did you do it?'

Killer: 'Do not compel me to recall bad things.'

Reporter: 'But she was your friend?'

Killer: 'I think I was possessed by madness . . . All I wanted was to live and die together with my beloved.'

Reporter: 'Are you thinking of your family, especially your sisters?'

Killer: 'I have stopped thinking about others and I just want to end my life. I am not in a position to think of all these things. Now, I have to look after myself only. Kindly do not ask me such things.'

There is one path, however, where a killer can in certain circumstances re-enter society without carrying the secret and at the same time achieve some form of personal redemption. In

1977 a Belfast man was sentenced to life imprisonment for the brutal murder of two people: a bus driver and a man driving a car with his young son. The killer was Kenny McClinton, who went on to become an evangelical pastor and an outspoken figure in Ulster loyalism. McClinton holds three postgraduate degrees: a Masters in theology, a PhD in philosophy and a further doctorate in literature. When in prison, McClinton underwent a religious conversion and became a born-again Christian. This mark of overt Christianity allows McClinton – and others like him – to be open about his violent past. The path to religion can become a killer's best friend, and it looks likely that Lorcan Bale has trodden this road.

At some point after his release from prison, it appears that Bale developed a more traditional religious fervour. How and why this happened, only he knows. His skills as an administrator have been put to wider use as a church officer, helping out with the day-to-day duties at a place of worship not far from his home. He has taken an interest in moral dilemmas, including organising an event questioning the ethical challenges facing those involved in genetic engineering. As secretary of a Christian church body, he plays a part in the planning of religious and social events within the community where he lives. As a church representative, he recently attended a public meeting on community policing where the discussion included a lively debate on police methods, progress on reducing the number of burglaries in the district and the ever-present problem of anti-social cycling. His has been quite an extraordinary journey, from a position in which society held him in contempt, to his present state: married with a steady job and an active church role. Not exactly a pillar of society, but not a pariah either.

Now, with over three decades having passed since the murder of John Horgan, should Lorcan Bale be left in peace to lead his life? Certainly those who need to know how he is conducting himself are already aware of where he lives and how he is managing his affairs. As a penal servitude prisoner, released on licence, he must check in once a year with the Irish authorities. In addition, he requires permission to live outside the jurisdiction. This is not uncommon and in such cases it is routine to inform the law enforcement authorities in the prisoner's chosen country of residence that there is a murderer released on licence now living on their patch. The authorities in the country where Lorcan Bale now lives are aware of his presence, and as long as he 'keeps his nose clean' he will not receive undue police attention.

We have maintained contact by phone and email, primarily to ensure that he is kept up to date with the press interest associated with this book. The deadline for delivering the finished manuscript was just a few days before my wedding. I contacted Lorcan Bale to let him know that I would be out of the country for three weeks on honeymoon and so would be unavailable to him, but contactable through my agents. This was a private exchange, unconnected with the murder of John Horgan, so it is not appropriate that his reply be quoted. But to briefly summarise it, he ignored the impact that publication of this book would have on him, instead picking up on the fact that I was to be married the next day. He offered his blessing and congratulations to both of us, saying it was important for us all to hear more about hope and about love.

It was a quite extraordinarily generous and surprising response. A great deal of time has passed since that shocking day in June almost four decades ago. The boy's killer has had ample time to reflect and perhaps atone. He has served his time, rebuilt his life and is making a contribution to society. A few days later, *The News of the World,* acting on information made public at the inquest, tracked down Bale and published his photo. My hope was that this would not happen but, journalism being a competitive business, it is hardly surprising that a well-known crime reporter seized upon a story that had landed at his feet. Perhaps now, as the story has been finally told, Lorcan Bale can be left alone to carry on with his life. Knocking at his door can achieve nothing and will in no way enhance the memory of John Horgan's short life.

The last word must go to the victims in this sorry affair. That Mr and Mrs Horgan have faced the loss of their only son with such dignity is a tribute to their faith and strength. And as for their little blue-eyed, fair-haired angel, who infected all who knew him with his winning smile, the inscription on his gravestone in Balgriffin Cemetery says it all:

'PAX IN AETERNUM'